WH Y
ELDERS?

*A BIBLICAL AND PRACTICAL
GUIDE FOR CHURCH MEMBERS*

BENJAMIN L. MERKLE

Kregel
Academic & Professional

Why Elders? A Biblical and Practical Guide for Church Members

© 2009 by Benjamin L. Merkle

Published by Kregel Publications, a division of Kregel, Inc., 2450 Oak Industrial Dr. NE, Grand Rapids, MI 49505.

ISBN 978-0-8254-3351-1

Printed in the United States of America
16 17 18 / 7 6 5 4

To all those who aspire
to the office of elder (overseer)
1 Timothy 3:1

Contents

Foreword

When Mark Dever and I joined up at Capitol Hill Baptist Church in Washington, D.C., in 1994, we had both seen the dark side of church government: power hungry deacons, unqualified elders, immoral pastors, distrusting congregations. It was enough to make anyone doubt the idea that "church" could ever work.

But one thing we could not do is ignore Scripture. There it was in black and white—words like *elders, deacons, above reproach, self-controlled, teach, preach,* and phrases like "keeping watch over your souls" (Heb. 13:17) and "entrust to faithful men who will be able to teach" (2 Tim. 2:2).

Maybe, just maybe, if we gave ourselves to building the church as outlined in Scripture, insisting on the right offices and the right people with the right character, we would see a new, deep, faithful, and lasting kind of health restored to Christ's church.

Fifteen years later I'm delighted to say that God has honored His Word as we have labored to obey it. We did not install a program, but we did install qualified, godly men as elders to do the work of shepherding God's flock. We did not lay hold of a high-tech management system, but we did lay hands on deacons who serve the church in countless ways and so grow the unity of the body.

Friend, this book is most likely in your hand because you have either run out of other things to try or you are simply determined (this time) to be biblical when it comes to leading your church. This book is an excellent place to start. Benjamin Merkle gives you a handy, readable primer on elders and deacons. You will have more questions after reading this, but you have to get this information down first.

Commit yourself to understanding the contents of this book. Commit yourself to being rigorously biblical. Commit yourself to gently leading your church. And then step back and watch what our faithful God does to prepare the bride of Christ for His return.

Matt Schmucker
Executive Director, 9Marks

Introduction

In recent years, the importance of having a biblical church organizational structure has become a central issue in many churches. Pastors study the New Testament and realize that their churches do not reflect what they find in Scripture. Church members likewise read their Bibles and wonder why their churches do not have elders or why the deacons rule the church instead of serve the church. In my opinion, this awareness is both a good sign and a bad sign. It is a good sign because it is healthy when God's people desire to be faithful and committed to His Word. The Bible should be our standard for all faith and practice. But it is also a bad sign because it reveals that we have drifted from God's model for the church and demonstrates that the church has lost confidence in the sufficiency of Scripture. Instead, we have patterned our churches after a successful, corporate model or a purely democratic model. Consequently, a return to a biblical model of government is desperately needed in the church today.

The organizational structure of a church is an important issue. It is not the most important issue, however. Many other issues have priority over this one: the deity of Christ; justification by faith alone; the inspiration, infallibility, and sufficiency of Scripture; and the substitutionary atonement are just a few examples of issues that are more crucial to the Christian faith. Moreover, although some aspects of church polity are clearly set forth in Scripture (e.g., teaching is the responsibility of the elders and not the deacons), other aspects are less clear (e.g., how church leaders should be selected). As a result, at certain points we must allow for some flexibility, knowing that our personal preferences should not be put on par with Scripture. It is necessary, therefore, that we approach the issue of church government with humility and with a teachable spirit.

But just because a topic may not be the most important does not make it unimportant. As we will see, the form of church government that a local congregation employs is extremely relevant to the life and health of the church. The church, as the body and bride of Christ, should seek to be pure and spotless. If certain biblical patterns and principles are ignored or abandoned, then the church will reap negative consequences. Therefore, it is beneficial for the church to follow the wisdom of God as recorded in Scripture.

Church government is important, not primarily because outward structures are important, but because outward structures directly affect who can be a leader in the church, what each leader does, and to whom each leader is accountable. Thus, when we speak of church government or church polity, we are really speaking of the roles, duties, and qualifications of those who lead the body of Christ. The following discussion represents a few reasons why church government is important.

IT AFFECTS WHO CAN BE A LEADER

One reason a biblical form of church government is desirable is that it directly affects who is qualified to lead or rule the church. Depending on the style of a church's polity, prospective leaders may or may not be held to the biblical requirements listed in 1 Timothy 3 and Titus 1. If a church emphasizes a candidate's professional accomplishments over his personal character and family life, it can result in the church of Jesus Christ being led by someone who is biblically unqualified. In other cases, a particular church may add qualifications to those listed in the New Testament. So, for example, in some churches a person will not be considered for leadership unless he has a minimum educational level (usually a Master of Divinity). Other relevant questions relate to whether a candidate must be a certain age or gender or whether a leader can be single, divorced, or remarried. Thus, a church's polity often determines who can be a leader.

The selection process of a leader also will differ depending on the church's organizational structure. In some congregations, leaders are chosen by the majority vote of the congregation. In other churches, the presiding leader or leaders are responsible for making the final decision of adding new staff members. Still, in other models, the bishop, who stands above the congregation, appoints a leader for the church. Therefore, a church's governmental structure relates not only to the qualifications needed to be a leader but also to the particular method by which a leader is selected.

IT AFFECTS WHAT A LEADER DOES

The organizational structure of a church also will affect the particular role of a church leader. This is important because the duties of a church leader have eternal consequences. Leaders, especially pastors or elders, are not merely responsible for running an organization but have the crucial role of shepherding, teaching, and equipping the congregation. In addition, church leaders are examples to the rest of the flock.

Church Leaders Are Shepherds

Having a biblical form of church government is important because church leaders are given the task of shepherding the congregation. The author of Hebrews exhorts his readers to obey their leaders and submit to them, "for they are keeping watch over your souls" (Heb. 13:17). What could be a more important and, at the same time, a more frightening job description? Leaders in the church (elders in particular) are given the task of making sure those in their charge have a healthy relationship with God. Their calling is not to run an organization or to help people maximize their potential in the world. Rather, their calling is to come beside their fellow brothers and sisters and lead them to the Great Shepherd.

But shepherds not only lead; they also must protect. In Acts 20, Paul warns the Ephesian elders that after he is gone, savage wolves will come in among them and will not spare the flock (v. 29). Godly church leaders are needed to shepherd the flock and to protect them against false teachers who would seek to lead the sheep astray.

Church Leaders Are Teachers

A second reason church government and, thus, church leaders are important is because they are given the task of teaching the congregation the Word of God. As such, it is crucial that those who teach the Word are adequately gifted and trained to accurately handle the Word of Truth (2 Tim.

2:15). The truth is always under attack. False teachers and false teachings are rampant outside and inside the church. Paul warned Timothy that certain false teachers have the devastating effect of "upsetting the faith of some" (v. 18), which means that some actually had abandoned the apostolic faith and embraced another gospel. It was for that very reason that Paul sent Timothy to Ephesus. Paul feared that false teachers were in danger of leading the congregation away from the pure gospel. But Paul not only sent Timothy to Ephesus and left Titus behind in Crete; he also sent letters to these associates (and to the churches they served) in order to protect the truth of the gospel. In a similar manner, church leaders are entrusted with the responsibility "to contend for the faith that was once for all delivered to the saints" (Jude 3). It is the elders of the church who are not only "to give instruction in sound doctrine" but also "to rebuke those who contradict it" (Titus 1:9).

Church Leaders Are Equippers

Paul writes that Christ gave gifts to the church, including apostles, prophets, evangelists, and pastor-teachers (Eph. 4:11). These leaders are given "to equip the saints for the work of ministry, for building up the body of Christ" (v. 12). Godly leaders are needed to equip the congregation to do the work of the ministry and to help the congregation become mature in their faith. Without such leaders, congregations are compared to children who are "tossed to and fro by the waves and carried about by every wind of doctrine, by human cunning, by craftiness in deceitful schemes" (v. 14). God has designed the body of Christ to be led by those who are gifted to help the congregation become stable and mature. Therefore, the specific roles given to leaders in the church are crucial for the body of Christ to reach maturity.

Church Leaders Are Examples

Because church leaders are examples to the congregation and those in their community, those who become leaders in the church have a great responsibility. Their testimony can either help or hurt the cause of Christ and His gospel. Peter exhorts the elders to be "examples to the flock" (1 Peter 5:3). The author of Hebrews encourages his readers to imitate the faith of their leaders (13:7). The type of church government a local congregation embraces often determines who their leaders are and what their leaders do. Because leaders are called to be examples to the flock and because the flock is encouraged to follow the example of their leaders, it becomes vital that a biblical model is used. Paul indicates that elders or overseers must not only manage their own households well but also must "be well thought of by outsiders" (1 Tim. 3:7). If a church's polity allows certain unqualified people to become leaders, their negative example will affect not only those in the church but also those outside the church, possibly causing some to despise the gospel.

IT AFFECTS TO WHOM A LEADER IS ACCOUNTABLE

The organizational structure of a church is also important because it determines to whom the church leaders are accountable. In some systems, the senior pastor is given unmatched authority and is accountable to no one in particular. Only a congregational vote is given more authority or power. In other models, the senior pastor is accountable to the deacons, who really are responsible for the business of the church. The senior pastor does only what the deacons tell him to do. Other structures do not have one leader but a number of leaders who are given equal authority. In this case, the pastor or minister is not accountable to the congregation but to other selected leaders who are on the church council. Finally, in some structures, the church leader does not report to the congregation, the deacons, or fellow council members but to the one who appointed him to his position. In this model, the church leader is accountable to someone outside the local congregation. Thus, the various forms of church government determine the accountability structure of the leaders.

CONCLUSION

The church as the body of Christ is composed of believers who have been redeemed by the precious blood of Christ. It is for this reason that those who are called to lead the church under God's guidance are given such an important task. Because the outward structure of a congregation directly relates to who leads the church, what a leader does, and to whom a leader is accountable, church government becomes an extremely important issue in the life and health of a church.

In my earlier book, *40 Questions About Elders and Deacons* (Kregel, 2008), I sought to answer the most important and relevant questions regarding the two offices of elder and deacon. *Why Elders?* is a summary of that work in a condensed format focusing specifically on the topic of why every church should have elders. These reasons are both biblical and practical. They are first biblical because the Bible is our standard for life and godliness (2 Peter 1:3), including how we organize our churches. But these reasons are also practical because God's way is always the best way—even though it may not be the easiest or most convenient path to follow. In the end (and even in the journey) it will prove to be full of blessings.

Chapter 1

It Is the Pattern of the New Testament Church

One of the strongest reasons churches should have elders is the fact that New Testament churches had elders. But before we discuss this consistent and widespread practice of calling leaders in the church "elders," we will first consider the various terms used to identify leaders in the church. Finally, we will think about the kind of authority elders should possess.

ELDERS AND TERMINOLOGY

Church leaders are given various titles in the New Testament. For example, leaders are called (1) elders, (2) overseers or bishops, (3) pastors or shepherds, and (4) deacons. Sometimes leaders are mentioned but are given no title. This phenomenon seems to be especially true during the earliest period of the church. In Galatians 6:6, Paul states, "One who is taught the word must share all good things with the one who teaches." In other words, it is the responsibility of those receiving instruction to provide for the physical sustenance of their teachers. This verse suggests that there was a class of instructors or catechizers who taught the Word to such an extent that they needed to be financially supported for their work. But if such people held a particular office, we are not told. In 1 Thessalonians 5:12–13, Paul exhorts the congregation: "We ask you, brothers, to respect those who labor among you and are over you in the Lord and admonish you, and to esteem them very highly in love because of their work." Here, Paul makes a distinction between the "brothers" and those they are to "respect" because of the work they do in teaching the congregation. No formal title is used, but it is clear that some were given positions of leadership in the church.

The author of Hebrews likewise makes a distinction between the leaders and those who should obey them: "Obey your leaders and submit to them, for they are keeping watch over your souls, as those who will have to give an account" (Heb. 13:17; cf. 13:7). If a leader must give an account, he needs to know not only that he is a leader (which implies some formal position recognized by the church) but also who he is accountable to lead (which implies a distinction between the leaders and the followers). Although we do not know what particular "office" these leaders may have held, we do know that the author has in mind a distinct group of individuals.

Elders and Overseers
By the time the Pastoral Epistles (1–2 Timothy, Titus) were written, however, it appears there were only two established

offices in the church—overseers/elders and deacons. Yet, overseers and deacons also were mentioned in Paul's earlier letter to the Philippians. In his opening greeting, he addresses "all the saints in Christ Jesus who are at Philippi, with the overseers and deacons" (Phil. 1:1). In 1 Timothy 3, Paul gives qualifications for the two offices. In verse 1 he writes, "If anyone aspires to the office of overseer, he desires a noble task." The following verses give the needed qualifications for those who might hold such an office. Then, in verse 8, Paul shifts to the office of deacon: "Deacons likewise must. . . ." Paul's letter to Titus, however, refers only to overseers, making no mention of deacons (Titus 1:5–9). This omission possibly indicates that the church in Crete was less developed than the church in Ephesus.

It also should be noted that the term *overseer* refers to the same office as that held by the person given the title "elder" (e.g., Acts 14:23; 1 Tim. 5:17). What New Testament evidence is there for viewing these two terms as synonymous?

Elder and *Overseer* Are Used Interchangeably

The first reason for seeing the terms *elder* and *overseer* as representing the same office is that the terms are used interchangeably. There are three texts that clearly demonstrate this usage (Acts 20:17, 28; Titus 1:5, 7; 1 Peter 5:1–2). Upon returning from his third missionary journey, Paul's ship harbored at Miletus for a few days. Knowing that he might not return to the region again, Paul decided to contact the leaders of the church at Ephesus. Luke informs us that Paul "sent to Ephesus and called the *elders* of the church to come to him" (Acts 20:17, emphasis added). After the elders arrive, Paul gives them a sort of "farewell speech." He exhorts them, "Pay careful attention to yourselves and to all the flock, in which the Holy Spirit has made you *overseers*, to care for the church of God" (20:28, emphasis added). Thus, in verse 17 Paul summons the "elders," but in verse 28 we read that the Holy Spirit made them "overseers." This usage demonstrates that the biblical writer did not make a distinction between the two terms.

Perhaps the most convincing passage that demonstrates that the terms *elder* and *overseer* are interchangeable is Titus 1:5–7. In verse 5, Paul writes to Titus, "This is why I left you in Crete, so that you might put what remained into order, and appoint *elders* in every town as I directed you" (emphasis added). When Paul gives the qualifications in verse 7, however, he replaces "elder" with "overseer." He continues, "For an *overseer*, as God's steward, must be . . ." (emphasis added).

A similar usage is found in 1 Peter 5:1–2. Peter, as a fellow elder, exhorts the elders of the churches. He writes, "I exhort the *elders* among you, as a fellow elder . . . shepherd the flock of God that is among you, serving as *overseers*" (my translation, emphasis added). Although this example is not as definitive since the verb form ("serving as overseers") is used (and not the noun "overseers"), it still emphasizes that the duty or function of the elders was to oversee the congregation. It would be strange if the elders are not the same people as those who were called "overseers" since they both perform the same duties.

Elders Are Never Given Separate Qualifications

A second factor that supports the view that the terms refer to the same office is that Paul never mentions the qualifications for elders. If elder and overseer are two separate offices, then it would seem reasonable to expect Paul to give the necessary qualifications for each office. In both 1 Timothy 3:1–7 and Titus 1:7–9, Paul gives the qualifications for anyone who aspires "to the office of overseer." But in both 1 Timothy

(5:17–20) and Titus (1:5) elders are also mentioned. If the offices are distinct, then what are the qualifications for someone to become an elder? This omission is especially telling because in 1 Timothy 5:22, Paul warns Timothy not to appoint someone to the office of elder too hastily since that position is to be filled only by qualified individuals (cf. 1 Tim. 4:14; 2 Tim. 1:6). If elder is a distinct office from overseer, we would expect the qualifications to be clearly stated for such an important position. What guidelines is Timothy to use in determining the moral and spiritual readiness of such a person? Is Timothy left to find his own way? No, Paul already has given Timothy the qualifications needed for someone to become an overseer (or elder) in the church. Although such arguments from silence are never conclusive, one wonders whether Paul would have ignored the requirements given the importance he attributes to the office.

Elders and Overseers Have the Same Function

A third reason for equating the two terms is that both elders and overseers have the same function—ruling/leading and teaching. For example, 1 Timothy 3:4–5 states that an *overseer* must "rule/manage" his own house before he is fit to "take care of" the church (cf. Rom. 12:8; 1 Thess. 5:12). Likewise, 1 Timothy 5:17 speaks of *elders* who "rule" well, indicating that all elders are involved in ruling or leading the church. In Acts 20:28, Paul charges the Ephesian *elders* to "oversee" and "shepherd" the church of God. Thus, both elders and overseers are given the task of ruling/leading the church.

In a similar manner, both also are given the duty of teaching the congregation. In 1 Timothy 3:2, every *overseer* must be "able to teach" in order to be qualified, and in Titus 1:9 an *overseer* must "be able to give instruction in sound doctrine and also to rebuke those who contradict it." Likewise, *elders* who rule well should be considered worthy of double honor, "especially those who labor in preaching and teaching" (1 Tim. 5:17). Because elders and overseers are given the same tasks of ruling/leading and teaching, they should be viewed as representing the same office.

Elders and Overseers Are Never Listed as Separate Offices

A final reason for equating the terms *elder* and *over-seer* is that nowhere in the New Testament are the three offices (elder, overseer, and deacon) mentioned together. This usage suggests that the three-tiered ecclesiastical system that later developed in many churches is foreign to the New Testament. Not until the second century—in the epistles of Ignatius—do we see a distinction between the overseer (i.e., the monarchical bishop) and the elders (i.e., presbytery). As such, Ignatius provides us with the first example of a three-tiered system with a bishop, a presbytery, and deacons (*To the Magnesians* 6:1). For Ignatius, the overseer is clearly distinct from the council of elders and is the sole head of the city-church. This later development, however, is not found in other writings of the post-apostolic era. For example, *1 Clement* (44:4–5) and the *Didache*, both probably written at the end of the first century, use the terms *elder* and *over-seer* interchangeably.

Elders and Pastors

Although the title "pastor" is commonly used in our modern church context, it is used only one time in the New Testament as a reference to a church leader. In Ephesians 4:11, we are told, "He [Jesus] gave the apostles, the prophets, the evangelists, the pastors and teachers." The term *pastor* is coupled with the term *teacher,* which together denote one order of ministry. In other words, the Greek construction favors interpreting this phrase as one office: the pastor/teacher. There is not one office of pastor and a separate office of teacher.

What, then, is the relationship between the office of pastor and that of the elder/overseer? Does "pastor" represent a separate and distinct office from that of the "elder" or "overseer"? There are at least two reasons to take these terms as representing the same office. First, elders/overseers are given the same tasks as pastors: shepherding and teaching. In Acts 20:17 we read that from Miletus Paul "sent to Ephesus and called the *elders* of the church to come to him" (emphasis added). After these elders come, Paul instructs them, "to shepherd [or 'pastor'] the church of God" (Acts 20:28, my translation). A similar passage is found in 1 Peter 5:1–3. In verse 1 Peter exhorts the "elders" of the churches. Then, in verse 2, he admonishes them to "shepherd the flock of God that is among you." According to these texts, the primary calling of an elder is to shepherd, or pastor, God's people.

Both elders/overseers and pastors are also given the task of teaching. In Ephesians 4:11, the term *pastor* is linked with the term *teacher,* indicating that the primary method a pastor shepherds his flock is through teaching them God's Word. Teaching is also the primary role of the elder/overseer. In 1 Timothy 3:2, a distinct qualification of the overseer is that he must be "able to teach." Later, Paul tells Timothy that the elders who rule well should be considered worthy of double honor, "especially those who labor in preaching and teaching" (1 Tim. 5:17). In a similar manner, Paul instructs Titus that an overseer must hold firm to the trustworthy Word he has been taught, "so that he may be able to give instruction in sound doctrine and also to rebuke those who contradict it" (Titus 1:9). Thus, because pastors and elders/overseers have the same function (i.e., shepherding and teaching), the two terms should be viewed as referring to the same office.

Second, as we mentioned earlier, the term *pastor* is found only once in the New Testament as a designation of a church leader. If this office is separate from the elder/overseer, what are the qualifications needed for those who hold this office? Paul gives us the qualifications for the elder/overseer but never for the pastor. Perhaps the reason for this omission is because in giving the qualifications for the elder/overseer, he is giving the qualifications for those who also can be called "pastor."

Elders and Titles

Finally, we will consider whether or not it is important to use the biblical titles. There are many churches that have leaders who essentially function as elders, but these leaders are not called "elders." Thus, the question before us is whether it is essential that each congregation employ this terminology or whether other terms will work just as well. I will seek to demonstrate that although the terminology used is not as important as the actual role of church leaders, there are good reasons for employing biblical terminology.

Titles Are Not Essential

Although titles are often used for church leaders, Jesus warns against seeking after them. In contrast to the scribes and Pharisees, Jesus instructs us, "But you are not to be called rabbi, for you have one teacher, and you are all brothers. And call no man your father on earth, for you have one Father, who is in heaven. Neither be called instructors, for you have one instructor, the Christ" (Matt. 23:8–10). There is a real danger of men seeking leadership in the church simply for the title or the recognition that the title brings. Jesus warns against such motivation by stating, "The greatest among you shall be your servant. Whoever exalts himself will be humbled, and whoever humbles himself will be exalted" (Matt. 23:11–12). Leadership in the church is not about acquiring titles but about becoming a servant.

The particular title used to describe a church leader is not the central issue. The more important issue is the role that person is playing. As we have seen, the apostle Paul sometimes uses titles to describe particular church leaders. It should be noted, however, that Paul is more interested in service than he is with any office. It is the one who *teaches* the Word who receives some sort of compensation (Gal. 6:6). It is those who *labor, lead,* and *admonish* who are to be respected *because of their work* (1 Thess. 5:12). The church is to be subject to those who *devote themselves to ministry* (1 Cor. 16:15–16). Epaphras is called a faithful *servant* who has *labored earnestly* for the gospel (Col. 1:7; 4:12). Archippus is exhorted to fulfill his *ministry* (Col. 4:17). Although at times Paul more specifically speaks of office (cf. Phil. 1:1; Eph. 4:11), his main concern is that the gospel is advanced. In one sense, then, titles are not essential to the Christian ministry. Paul emphasizes the importance of a leader's function more than the particular title a leader bears.

Titles Are Important

Simply because titles are not essential to the Christian ministry, however, does not mean they have no importance or relevance. Some churches purposefully avoid the biblical terminology because it is perceived as possibly being divisive. Some people in the church prefer one title, while others prefer another. To stay clear of any controversy, all biblical titles are avoided. Other churches simply use the titles that have been passed down from one generation to another, giving no thought to whether such titles are accurate. Thus, the tradition of the church or denomination takes precedence over the biblical usage of the terms. Yet, there are at least three reasons why I believe it is beneficial for churches to faithfully use the titles given in Scripture.

Before I go into the various reasons why certain titles should be used, it is necessary to first explain that the title itself, without the appropriate role, is counterproductive. For example, the office of deacon is consistently found in many churches, although the duties of deacons vary widely. In many churches, the deacons function like elders in the sense that they are involved in leading and shepherding the church. In other circumstances, the deacons do not really serve but are simply elected or chosen to make important decisions. In some denominations, a deacon is an entry-level ministerial position that is the first step up the ecclesiastical ladder.

The office of elder is more complex due to the number of terms that can be used. Which title is to be preferred: elder, overseer, bishop, or pastor? Here we must allow for some flexibility because the Bible does not employ one term consistently. While the title "elder" is more common than "overseer," both refer to the same officeholder and therefore can be used. If the title "pastor" is used, it should be used consistently. That is, it is best not to make a distinction between "elders" and "pastors." The title "bishop" has the same essential meaning as "overseer," but it is often avoided by evangelical churches due to the later connotations the term took on. This is also why most modern English Bible versions prefer to translate the Greek term *episkopos* "overseer" rather than "bishop."

The first reason it is helpful for church leaders to use the terms as they are used in Scripture is that it bases our authority on the Bible and not human wisdom. By using titles that are not found in Scripture, the congregation may begin to doubt the basis of authority for the church leaders. But when it is shown that elders or overseers are responsible for shepherding and teaching the church based on the model of the New Testament churches, it gives authority and credibility to their office. Many churches today model their organizational structure after a successful business model. The church, however, should not be run like a business, and it is dangerous to organize the church based on whatever works in society. God has provided the church with a basic structure that should be closely followed. To stray from that structure is, in a sense, to say that man's way is better than God's way. By using the terminology along with the appropriate roles, the leaders communicate to the congregation that the Bible is the final authority for all faith and practice.

A second reason it is best to use the titles for leaders given in Scripture is that it allows the congregation to know what to expect from the leadership. If other terms are used, the congregation either has to guess what the responsibilities of the leaders are or read their individual job descriptions (which they may or may not have access to). If the biblical terms and functions are used, however, the congregation will know immediately that the deacons are not in charge of preaching and teaching or ruling the church. Rather, they are responsible for the menial and service-oriented tasks of the church.

Finally, it is beneficial to use the biblical terminology for church leaders because it holds leaders to the biblical qualifications. If the ruling and teaching leaders of the church are simply called "council members," or are given some other title not found in Scripture, then it is difficult to hold such leaders to the biblical qualifications. When one of them is questioned as to whether he meets the qualifications for elders or deacons, he can simply reply, "You cannot hold me to those qualifications because I am not an elder or a deacon. I am a council member." If the qualifications are going to be consistently applied to the leaders of the church, it is best for those leaders to bear the title given at the beginning of the qualifications. If the appropriate titles are not used, it confuses the congregation and provides a way of escape for unqualified officeholders. Using the titles found in Scripture avoids such confusion. And, as church members read their Bibles and the qualifications given therein, they just might begin to examine their own hearts to see how they measure up to such a standard. If they aspire to hold a particular office, they will know precisely what is expected of them based on the qualifications given in Scripture.

ELDERS AND PLURALITY

The concept of shared leadership is a common theme in the Bible. In the Old Testament, leadership was shared by the elders of Israel. In the New Testament, Jesus chose twelve apostles to lead the church. In addition, the early church appointed seven men to assist the apostles by caring for the church's widows (Acts 6:1–6). This pattern of plurality was continued with the establishment of the Christian eldership.

Elders and the New Testament Church

The first mention of Christian elders appears in Acts 11:30, which tells us the church in Antioch sent Barnabas and Paul to the elders in Jerusalem with money to aid in the famine relief. Later, in Acts 15, the elders are referenced along with the apostles in the context of the Jerusalem Council. Similar to the apostles, the elders formed a collective body of leadership.

On Paul's first missionary journey, he and Barnabas preached the gospel in Asia Minor, especially in the cities of Antioch, Iconium, Lystra, and Derbe. On their return trip, Luke records that they "appointed elders for them in every church" (Acts 14:23). In this verse we are specifically told that a plurality of elders was appointed in every church. Although the church was recently established, Paul and Barnabas believed it was important for each church to possess more than one spiritual leader. Even though Luke mentions Barnabas and Paul appointing "elders" only in Acts 14:23, it is likely that this was Paul's customary procedure.

At the end of his third missionary journey, Paul summoned "the elders of the church to come to him" (Acts 20:17). Together, these elders were exhorted "shepherd the church of God" (Acts 20:28 NASB). The church in Ephesus is referred to in the singular (it is *not* the church*es* of Ephesus), indicating there was only one body of believers in Ephesus that was governed by a plurality of leaders (though it is likely the church consisted of a number of house groups).

Luke's record in Acts fits well with Paul's own account that each church was led by a plurality of elders. He writes to young Timothy, "Let the elders who rule well be considered worthy of double honor, especially those who labor in preaching and teaching" (1 Tim. 5:17). When Paul writes to the church at Philippi, he specifically greets the "overseers and deacons" (Phil. 1:1). Although the term for elder is not used in this context, we have already demonstrated that the terms for elder and overseer referred to the same group of people. Later, Paul directed Titus to "appoint elders in every town" (Titus 1:5). At the end of his ministry, Paul still believed in the necessity of establishing a body of elders in the local church.

The practice of having a plurality of elders is consistently found in the other writings of the New Testament as well. James, the Lord's brother, raises the question, "Is anyone among you sick?" His answer is, "Let him call for the elders of the church, and let them pray over him, anointing him with oil in the name of the Lord" (James 5:14). Again, we should note the sick person is to call for the "elders" (plural) of the "church" (singular). Finally, the apostle Peter exhorts the "elders" among the believers scattered throughout Pontus, Galatia, Cappadocia, Asia, and Bithynia (1 Peter 5:1).

In almost every reference in the New Testament, the term for "elders" is found in the plural. There are a few exceptions, however. In 1 Timothy 5:19, Paul states, "Do not admit a charge against an elder except on the evidence of two or three witnesses." In this verse the singular form is used, not because the church in Ephesus had only one elder, but because the context refers to accusations brought up against an individual elder. Verse 17 clearly mentions that there was a plurality of elders in the Ephesian church. The other two occurrences of the singular form occur in the later two epistles of John where John describes himself as "the elder" (2 John 1; 3 John 1). In this case, the singular must be used because the title is used as a personal designation (cf. 1 Peter 5:1, where Peter calls himself a "fellow elder").

There are also other terms used to describe the plurality of leaders in the church. Paul urges the Corinthians to "be subject" to the household of Stephanas "and to every fellow worker and laborer" (1 Cor. 16:15–16). In his first letter to the church at Thessalonica, Paul exhorts the believers "to respect those who labor among you and are over you in the Lord and admonish you" (1 Thess. 5:12). Although the term for "elders" is not used, it is clear that those whom Paul is referring to were the spiritual leaders of the congregation, performing elder-like functions. Finally, the author of Hebrews also indicates that the church to which he writes was led by a plurality of shepherds. In Hebrews 13:7, the author states, "Remember your leaders, those who spoke to you the word of God. Consider the outcome of their way of life, and imitate their faith." He then exhorts the congregation, writing, "Obey your leaders and submit to them, for they are keeping watch over your souls, as those who will have to give an account" (Heb. 13:17). In the closing of his letter, he adds, "Greet all your leaders and all the saints" (Heb. 13:24). In each case, the author refers to a plurality of leaders.

The New Testament evidence indicates that every church had a plurality of elders. There is no example in the New Testament of one elder or pastor leading a congregation as the sole or primary leader. There was a plurality of elders at the churches in Jerusalem (Acts 11:30), Antioch of Pisidia, Lystra, Iconium, and Derbe (Acts 14:23), Ephesus (Acts 20:17; 1 Tim. 5:17); Philippi (Phil. 1:1), the cities of Crete (Titus 1:5), the churches in the dispersion to which James wrote (James 5:14), the Roman provinces of Pontus, Galatia, Cappadocia, Asia, and Bithynia (1 Peter 1:1), and possibly the church(es) to which Hebrews was written (Heb. 13:7, 17, 24).

How many elders should each congregation have? The Bible never identifies a specific number of elders that should lead each local congregation. Up to this point we argued that a plurality, at least two elders, was the pattern of the earliest congregations. Apart from having a plurality, we are left to use godly wisdom and common sense in the selection of elders. There are a number of important factors to remember.

First, it is important that every elder has a strong desire to serve in that capacity. Paul informs us that it is a noble task if someone aspires to the office of elder (1 Tim. 3:1). Likewise, Peter informs us that elders should shepherd God's flock not from compulsion, but willingly (1 Peter 5:2). One should not agree to serve as an elder out of guilt, because he was nominated, or because he received the most votes. To be effective, an elder must love and enjoy the hard work of being a shepherd. Second, we must remember that eldership is a calling. Paul tells the elders of the Ephesian church, "Pay careful attention to yourselves and to all the flock, *in which the Holy Spirit has made you overseers*" (Acts 20:28, emphasis added). Paul may have appointed and installed these men to their office, but ultimately it was God who raised them up to serve in His church. Likewise, we read in Paul's letter to the Ephesian church that the ascended Christ "gave some to be . . . pastors and teachers" (Eph. 4:11 NKJV). Pastors, or elders, are a gift from Christ to His church. Therefore, from one perspective, a church should appoint as many elders as God gives to a local congregation. Third, an elder does not have to be in a full-time or even a paid church position. An elder can have a "secular" job and still be effective in shepherding people in the congregation, as long as he is diligent, faithful, and has a calling from God. Fourth, every candidate must meet the qualifications before he is eligible to serve as elder. *How many* elders is not as important as *who* the elders are.

Elders and Staff

What is the relationship between staff members and elders? Is every staff member automatically an elder? Is the pastor also considered an elder? Let me offer a few suggestions or principles that will help us think biblically about these questions.

Not All Staff Members Are Elders

Sometimes churches classify all staff members as elders since they serve the church in a full-time capacity. But simply because someone is hired by the church to perform a certain leadership function does not mean that person should be counted among the elders. Each staff member must meet the qualifications listed in the New Testament before he can serve as an elder (1 Tim. 3:1–7; Titus 1:5–9). For example, if a staff member is not "able to teach," he is disqualified from being an elder. Also, staff members who are not involved in shepherding the congregation—a primary task of a pastor—also should not be counted among the elders. A staff member also may be too young or too inexperienced to be trusted with responsibilities of eldership. If someone is not respected by the congregation, then it would be counterproductive to install him to the office of elder. It is also not wise to use terms such as "youth pastor" for someone who is not an elder. Again, such usage confuses the biblical teaching because "elder" and "pastor" refer to the same office. Thus, to call someone who is not an elder a youth (or children's, singles', young adult, etc.) pastor is misleading.

Not All Elders Are Staff Members
We must also note that while not all staff members should be elders, not all elders should be staff members. That is, it is unhealthy to limit those who can serve as elders to those who are employed by the church. This unbiblical distinction divides the congregation into professional clergy who do the ministry and the laity who support the ministry. Instead, it is better to leave the eldership open to anyone who is qualified to serve—whether they are on staff or not. To exclude non-staff members from serving as elders deprives the church of capable and qualified leaders. Excluding non-staff members from eldership also can lead to instability in leadership when a staff member accepts a position in another church. Each time a pastor leaves, the church undergoes a difficult crisis as the church is left without leadership. Consequently, it is

healthy for a church to have more non-staff elders than staff elders. This helps protect the church from being overly dependent on paid staff. Ideally, there would be a minimum of three elders: one staff elder and two non-staff elders. On the other hand, the board of elders probably should not be so large that separate committees are needed to study issues or make important decisions (such as an executive committee). Not subdividing the eldership simplifies the authority structure and helps avoid unnecessary divisions.

Some Staff Members Should Be Elders

In other congregations, virtually no staff members are among the eldership. In some cases, the senior pastor is the only staff member who is an elder. This model also is not ideal because it also tends to create an unbiblical distinction between paid staff and unpaid leaders and creates a third office in the church. In addition to pastors and deacons, the third office of elder is added. But as demonstrated earlier, the terms *pastor* and *elder* refer to the same office.

Don't Distinguish Between Staff Elders and Non-Staff Elders

Having a staff-led church often leads to alienation of the congregation from their pastors/staff. The full-time paid leaders in the church are hired professionals who usually come from other churches. The congregation considers it the responsibility of the paid staff to do the work of the ministry. In order to overcome this separation and alienation, some churches have attempted to institute a "lay-elder" system. These lay elders are given some responsibility in the church but are still separate and distinct from the pastoral staff. This is an attempt by the pastoral staff to provide some leadership in the church that does not leave the congregation feeling isolated from the professional staff members. This particular system, however, has a number of problems. First, it still maintains a distinction between the professional and nonprofessional leaders. The professional staff still run the church and make most of the important decisions. Second, it introduces an unbiblical distinction between "pastors" and "elders." Therefore, to make a distinction between pastors who are paid staff members who run the church on a daily basis and elders who are unpaid non-staff members is to create an office that is not found in the Bible. It is not wrong, of course, to have paid and unpaid workers in the church. What is not recommended, however, is to give unpaid elders less authority in the church by creating a distinct office. The titles "lay elder" and "lay pastor" confuse the biblical teaching and are better left unused.

ELDERS AND AUTHORITY

The New Testament does not tell us precisely how much authority the elders of the local congregation should have. We have to take relevant texts from the New Testament and attempt to synthesize the principles that are taught in each text. As a result, we must be cautious of conclusions that are too rigid or dogmatic. The principles we gather from Scripture should be followed, but the outworking of these principles can be appropriated in different ways.

Elders Have Authority

In the first place, we must note that the Bible is clear that elders have authority. Paul writes to the congregation in Thessalonica, "We ask you, brothers, to respect those who labor among you and are over you in the Lord and admonish you" (1 Thess. 5:12). This text demonstrates that in the earliest stage of the church, there were some who were set apart as leaders and, as such, were to be respected because of their important work in the church. Paul makes a distinction between the "brothers" and those whom they are to respect. Apparently, not every believer was to be honored and respected in the same way. Some, because of their gifts and function in the community, were to be considered worthy of special recognition. This text is thus similar to 1 Timothy 5:17, where Paul states, "Let the elders who rule well be considered worthy of double honor, especially those who labor in preaching and teaching." Just as elders have authority in their homes, so also they have authority in the church (1 Tim. 3:4–5).

Another text that demonstrates the authority of the elders is found at the end of the book of Hebrews. The author urges the congregation, "Obey your leaders and submit to them, for they are keeping watch over your souls, as those who will have to give an account" (Heb. 13:17). Although elders are not mentioned, it is safe to assume that the "leaders" who possessed this type of authority were indeed elders. Similarly, Paul encourages the Corinthian believers to submit to the household of Stephanas, as well as other fellow workers (1 Cor. 16:15–16; cf. 1 Peter 5:5). Those who lead the church must be servant leaders, however—ones the congregation will gladly submit to.

The very functions or duties of the elders communicate that their office carries with it a certain amount of authority. As teachers, they are charged with the task of authoritatively proclaiming God's Word. They are not merely offering suggestions or voicing their own opinions but are declaring, "Thus says the Lord." Consequently, the congregation has the duty to obey their words, not because they are the words of the preacher but the words of God, insomuch as the preacher accurately and faithfully conveys the gospel message.

As shepherds, the elders are given the task of leading

God's people (Acts 20:28; Eph. 4:11; 1 Peter 5:2). If some are leading as shepherds, the assumption is that others are following their leadership. Of course, with the authority given to the shepherd also comes added responsibility. He must guide, watch over, and protect those in his flock. He is even called to go after wandering sheep and to bring them back into the fold. Elders are accountable before God for their role as shepherds (Heb. 13:17). In the same way, the sheep are accountable before God to obey and follow the shepherds so that they can fulfill their responsibilities with joy (Heb. 13:17).

As representatives, the elders speak and act on behalf of the entire congregation. When Barnabas and Paul brought famine relief money on behalf of the church in Antioch, it was received by the elders of the Jerusalem church (Acts 11:30). Later, as Paul was journeying to Jerusalem from Greece, he briefly harbored at Miletus. There he called for the elders of the Ephesian church to come to him so that he might encourage them (Acts 20:17). Although his concern was for the whole church, he called the elders because they served as the leaders and representatives of the church.

The authority of the eldership comes from God and not the congregation. Although the congregation affirms the elders' calling and authority, theirs is an authority with a divine origin. Paul tells the Ephesian elders that the Holy Spirit made them overseers (Acts 20:28). They were called and given authority by God and not by man. Yet, it was probably the Ephesian congregation that endorsed them and Paul then appointed them publicly to their office. In the letter to the Ephesians, Paul states that Christ has given gifts to the church, including pastor-teachers (Eph. 4:11). Therefore, the authority of an elder does not come from the congregation but from Christ Himself.

Elders Have Limited Authority

It must be pointed out, however, that the elders' authority is not absolute. They derive authority from the Word of God, and when they stray from that Word, they abandon their God-given authority. As an apostle of Jesus Christ, Paul possessed nearly unmatched authority. Yet Luke tells us that the Bereans were nobler than others because they not only received the preached Word with eagerness, but they also examined the Scriptures daily to see if Paul indeed spoke the truth (Acts 17:11). Paul himself states that even if he or an angel preached a gospel other than the true gospel, "let him be accursed" (Gal. 1:8). The authority that the elders possess is not so much found in their office but in the duties they perform (and the Christlike character they display). Elders are not to be obeyed simply because they are elders. Rather, they are to be obeyed because they have the responsibility of shepherding and teaching the congregation. They shepherd because the Word calls upon elders to shepherd. They teach because the Word calls upon elders to teach. But when their shepherding and teaching stray from Scripture, their authority as shepherds and teachers is no longer binding on the congregation.

In addition, the authority of the elders did not extend beyond the local church. There is no evidence in the New Testament that elders exercised authority outside their own congregation (in distinction from apostles, who appear to have had authority over multiple congregations). As shepherds, they ministered to their flock, but once they ventured outside their community to another congregation, they no longer functioned authoritatively.

The Congregation Has Final Authority

The authority of elders is balanced by the authority of the congregation as a whole. It is important to remember, however, that Jesus Christ and His Word have ultimate authority in the church. Everything should be done under His authority because he is "the head of the body, the church" (Col. 1:18). But, while acknowledging Jesus' lordship, who makes the final decisions in the church? Again, no answer is explicitly given to us in the Bible. Historically, however, congregationalists have given final authority to the congregation. There is strong New Testament evidence for this conclusion. The New Testament seems to favor a self-governing model of the church. In the early church, many important decisions—such as selecting leaders (Acts 1:23; 6:2–3), sending missionaries (Acts 13:3; 14:27), determining theological positions (Acts 15:22), deciding church discipline (Matt. 18:17), and performing excommunication (1 Cor. 5:2)—were the responsibilities of the local congregation. Additional support is found in the fact that Paul's letters to churches were addressed to entire congregations and not just to officeholders in the church. Finally, the priesthood of all believers and the teaching of Jesus also lend evidence in favor of congregationalism (1 Peter 2:5, 9; Rev. 1:6; 5:10; 20:6).

Thus, key decisions in the church should not be given only to the elders but should be brought before the entire congregation. Because the church is a body (and not merely a head or feet), all in the church are important and should be allowed to be a part of major decisions. In saying this, two items need to be stressed. First, the elders are the leaders in the church and should therefore be given freedom to lead. Every decision should not be brought before the church. Important decisions, such as the addition of a new elder or deacon, the budget, and a change to the constitution or bylaws, are congregational matters. Most other areas of concern, however, should be left to the leadership of the elders and deacons. It is not usually beneficial for a church to let all the members vote on what color the carpet should be.

Second, if the church uses the democratic method of voting, then it *must* practice church discipline and have a regenerate church membership. If church discipline is not practiced, then those who should no longer be members of the church will be allowed to vote. If someone is living in open, unrepentant rebellion against God, that person should be removed from the membership (1 Cor. 5:2). To give such a person the privilege of voting is unwise. Furthermore, those who do not attend the church on a regular basis (for reasons other than health) also should be removed from membership. If they are not an active part of the church community, they do not need to be deciding important matters related to the life of the church. If such people are not removed from membership, the church will find people who have not attended a worship service for many years attending the business meetings and voting on important and controversial issues.

CONCLUSION

Every church should have elders because New Testament churches had elders. Sometimes these leaders were called "overseers" or "pastors/shepherds" (all three of these terms—*elder, overseer, pastor*—refer to the same office and were used interchangeably in the New Testament). Although I believe a biblical title should be used, the most important issue is not the title that is used but rather the character of the person and the role he performs. The overwhelming evidence in the New Testament is that every congregation was led by a group of elders and not merely by a single pastor. These elders consisted of those who received pay because of their hard work and those who served as volunteers. While elders do have authority to lead the church—and should be given such authority by the congregation—final authority resides in the congregation as a whole.

Chapter 2

It Provides Help and Accountability for a Pastor

A second reason every church should have elders relates to the important and difficult duties a pastor is called to perform. Because of these responsibilities, a pastor needs others who can share this burden. In addition, having elders provides mutual accountability for those who lead the church. To effectively hold each other accountable, each elder/pastor must have equal authority.

ELDERS AND THEIR DUTIES

In the contemporary church, elders, or pastors, are busier than ever. With so many programs, committees, and events, it is often hard to find time to meet the needs of the congregation. Some view the pastor as the CEO, while others view him as an employee. Still others view the pastor as their personal therapist who has the answers to all their problems. With so many responsibilities vying for a pastor's time, what should take precedence? In other words, what is the main duty or role of an elder? There are at least four primary duties of an elder that should not be ignored. The elder is called to be (1) a leader, (2) a shepherd, (3) a teacher, and (4) an equipper.

Elder as Leader

First of all, an elder is called to lead the church. He is not just a leader in the church, but he is called, with the other elders, to lead the church. Paul writes that an elder "must manage his own household well," and then adds the reason, "for if someone does not know how to manage his own household, how will he care for God's church?" (1 Tim. 3:4–5). The analogy Paul makes is between the role of the husband and the role of the elder. If an elder cannot manage (rule/lead/ care for) his own family, then how can he be expected to take on the additional responsibilities and challenges of leading the church? Later, Paul writes, "Let the elders who rule well be considered worthy of double honor" (1 Tim. 5:17). It is evident, then, that one of the main functions of an elder is to lead the church (cf. Rom. 12:8).

Similarly, the author of Hebrews instructs the congregation, "Obey your leaders and submit to them" (Heb. 13:17; cf. 1 Thess. 5:12). The leaders, probably the elders, thus have a certain authority. Authority in the church is not equally divided among the members. And yet nowhere are the leaders told to force the congregation to submit to them. That is because leadership in the church must be humble leadership that leads by example. A pastor should not ask people to do something he himself is not willing to do. Peter encourages the elders to lead the people in a way that is not domineering, "being examples to the flock" (1 Peter 5:3). The author of Hebrews writes, "Remember your leaders, those who spoke to you the word of God. Consider the outcome of their way of life, and imitate their faith" (Heb. 13:7).

Biblical leadership is humble, servant leadership. Jesus gave the perfect example of humility when he washed the feet of His disciples (John 13:1–20). Jesus explained this symbolic act to His disciples: "Do you understand what I have done to you? You call me Teacher and Lord, and you are right, for so I am. If I then, your Lord and Teacher, have washed your feet, you also ought to wash one another's feet. For I have given you an example, that you also should do just as I have done to you" (John 13:12–15). What does a humble leader look like? First of all, a humble leader does not demand respect. He realizes that his position in the church is a gift from God and that the church itself is God's church. A humble leader also is teachable. He admits that he does not have all the answers but is willing to listen and learn from others. Furthermore, he is willing to work with others because he realizes the importance of teamwork and accountability. A humble leader is also a servant. When James and John asked if they could sit at Jesus' right and left hand side in heaven, Jesus said to His disciples, "You know that those who are considered rulers of the Gentiles lord it over them, and their great ones exercise authority over them. But it shall not be so among you. But whoever would be great among you must be your servant, and whoever would be first among you must be slave of all" (Mark 10:42–44). Finally, and most importantly, a humble leader does all to the glory of God (1 Cor. 10:31).

Elder as Shepherd

As we already demonstrated, the title "pastor" (Eph. 4:11) is simply another term used to describe an elder or overseer, and "pastor" has the same meaning as "shepherd." Because the people of God are referred to figuratively as "sheep," those who tend to their needs and exercise leadership over them are figuratively called "shepherds." Peter exhorts the elders to "shepherd the flock of God that is among you" (1 Peter 5:2). Thus, the elders lead the people of God as a shepherd leads a flock of sheep. This is a significant analogy. Church leaders are not cowboys who drive the sheep. Rather, they are caring shepherds who lead and protect the sheep. Furthermore, the shepherd's primary task is not to run an organization but to care for people's souls. A pastor is not primarily a motivator, administrator, or program facilitator but a shepherd.

In the Old Testament, the Lord rebuked the leaders of Israel for not being good shepherds. The basic charge against these leaders was that they looked after their own interests and ignored the needs of the sheep. We read in Ezekiel, "Ah, shepherds of Israel who have been feeding yourselves! Should not shepherds feed the sheep? You eat the fat, you clothe yourselves with wool, you slaughter the fat ones, but you do not feed the sheep. The weak you have not strengthened, the sick you have not healed, the injured you have not bound up, the stray you have not brought back, the lost you have not sought, and with force and harshness you have ruled them" (Ezek. 34:2–4).

Jesus, of course, is the perfect Shepherd. He is the Good Shepherd who "lays down his life for the sheep" (John 10:11; cf. John 15:13). He is the one who always feeds His sheep. He strengthens them, heals them, binds their wounds, and brings back those who are straying. Peter therefore describes Jesus as "the Shepherd and Overseer" of our souls (1 Peter 2:25). He is the "chief Shepherd" (1 Peter 5:4) who is the perfect example for those who are undershepherds.

The shepherd must be willing to protect the sheep. Paul warns the Ephesian elders in his farewell speech, "Pay careful attention to yourselves and to all the flock, in which the Holy Spirit has made you overseers, to care for the church of God, which he obtained with his own blood. I know that after my departure fierce wolves will come in among you, not sparing the flock" (Acts 20:28–29). A good shepherd will pay close attention to the flock and protect the sheep from wolves that would seek to harm them spiritually.

Often, however, sheep get injured and need assistance. It is therefore important for the elders to attend to the needs of those in the congregation. They need to visit not only those who are spiritually sick or weak but also those who are physically sick. James raises the question, "Is anyone among you sick?" His answer for this problem is, "Let him call for the elders of the church, and let them pray over him, anointing him with oil in the name of the Lord" (James 5:14). Isaiah gives us a picture of a good shepherd as he explains how the Lord God shepherds His people: "He will tend his flock like a shepherd; he will gather the lambs in his arms; he will carry them in his bosom, and gently lead those that are with young" (Isa. 40:11). In giving the needed qualifications for an elder, Paul states that he must be able to manage his own household well or else he will not be able to "care for" God's church (1 Tim. 3:4–5). The Greek word translated "care for" is found only two other times in the New Testament, both in the parable of the Good Samaritan. We are told that the Good Samaritan had compassion on the injured Jew, cleaning and binding his wounds. He then set the dying man on his animal and brought him to the inn and "took care of him" (Luke 10:34). The Samaritan then commands the innkeeper, "Take care of him" (Luke 10:35). It is this type of care that the shepherds of God's church are called to display in their lives and in their ministries.

Shepherding carries with it a great responsibility before God. The sheep are placed under the care of the shepherd. The sheep have the responsibility to follow the shepherd, but the shepherd has to be diligent in keeping watch over the sheep. The author of Hebrews exhorts his readers, "Obey your leaders and submit to them, for they are keeping watch over your souls, as those who will have to give an account" (Heb. 13:17). Thus, the reason the congregation is to follow the leadership of the elders is because they are given the task of watching over their souls—a responsibility for which they will be held accountable.

A major way in which elders shepherd the congregation is through prayer. The apostles appointed the Seven to help serve tables so that they (the apostles) could devote themselves "to prayer and to the ministry of the word" (Acts 6:4). If we truly believe Paul when he states that we do not "wrestle against flesh and blood, but against . . . the spiritual forces of evil in the heavenly places" (Eph. 6:12), then we will be dedicated to "praying at all times" (Eph. 6:18). It is clear that prayer is a primary calling of the elders. James states, "Is anyone among you sick? Let him call for the elders of the church, and let them pray over him" (James 5:14). But certainly the prayer of elders should not be limited to those who are sick. Elders also should be praying that those under their care will be fruitful in their Christian lives—that they will be faithful in their marriages, raise their children with wisdom, and share the gospel with their families, coworkers, and neighbors.

Elder as Teacher

It is clear from the New Testament that an elder is primarily a teacher. The elders' calling to lead the church through their teaching is what distinguishes them from the deacons.

A unique qualification for an elder is that he must be "able to teach" (1 Tim. 3:2). A few chapters later Paul mentions that those who rule well are worthy of double honor, that is, those who work hard at "preaching and teaching" (1 Tim. 5:17). In Titus, Paul describes this role in more detail. He explains that an elder "must hold firm to the trustworthy word as taught, so that he may be able to give instruction in sound doctrine and also to rebuke those who contradict it" (Titus 1:9). Paul indicates that the goal of teaching is not only to encourage believers by giving them biblical instruction but also to firmly rebuke those who oppose the truth of the gospel. The teaching role is also inseparably connected to the function of the pastor when Paul states that God has gifted the church with "pastors and teachers," or pastor-teachers (Eph. 4:11).

There are other texts that associate the role of church leaders with teaching. Although elders or overseers are not specifically mentioned in the following examples, it is likely that those who were doing the teaching were in fact elders. Paul reminds the churches in Galatia that the "one who is taught the word must share all good things with the one who teaches" (Gal. 6:6). Two things should be observed in this verse. First, that which was being taught was the Word. This emphasis on the Word of God was evident from the beginning of the church. We read that the first believers in Jerusalem "devoted themselves to the apostles' teaching" (Acts 2:42). Second, some were so dedicated to the task of teaching that they required financial support. Though not named elders, these people were performing the function of elders among those in the congregation. In 1 Thessalonians 5:12, Paul exhorts the congregation "to respect those who labor among you and are over you in the Lord and admonish you." These leaders who are to be respected are described as those who "labor," "are over," and "admonish" the

Thessalonian Christians. Most likely, those who were entrusted to lead and teach (i.e., admonish) the congregation were the elders. Likewise, in Hebrews 13:7, the leaders are defined as "those who spoke . . . the word of God" to the church. This text is most likely referring to the teaching ministry of the elders.

Paul also stresses the importance of the teaching ministry to his associate Timothy. Although it is incorrect to view Timothy as the "pastor" of the church at Ephesus because he carried more authority as Paul's apostolic delegate, it is clear that his role overlapped that of the elders. Paul tells his protégé Timothy, "Devote yourself to the public reading of Scripture, to exhortation, to teaching" (1 Tim. 4:13). The reading and subsequent exposition of the Bible was at the heart and center of the worship service. For Timothy to neglect this task would be a colossal failure on his part. In 2 Timothy, Paul's last letter in the Bible, Paul realizes that his death is imminent, and he senses the urgency to once again encourage his son in the faith, Timothy. With the utmost solemnity and seriousness, Paul writes, "I charge you in the presence of God and of Christ Jesus, who is to judge the living and the dead, and by his appearing and his kingdom: preach the word; be ready in season and out of season; reprove, rebuke, and exhort, with complete patience and teaching" (2 Tim. 4:1–2). The importance of solid, gospel teaching in the church is vital to the church's existence. The Word must be preached, and it is the task of elders to preach that Word (cf. Acts 6:4).

Elder as Equipper

The role of the elder as teacher is important, not just for the health of the church in the present, but also for the growth of the church in the future. As a result, it is not enough for the elders to simply be teachers; they also must be purposefully equipping the next generation of elders to minister alongside them or to plant new churches in the community. Too often I have witnessed pastors who preach and teach year after year but, when all is said and done, they have effectively trained and equipped nobody to take their place. It is a sign of an unhealthy church if there is no one in the congregation who can step into the gap and fill the pulpit whenever the pastor is gone. Biblical eldership includes training others to do the task of preaching and teaching.

Again, Paul's words to Timothy are instructive. He tells Timothy, "What you have heard from me in the presence of many witnesses entrust to faithful men who will be able to teach others also" (2 Tim. 2:2). As Paul's faithful coworker, Timothy was entrusted with the task of passing on the pure gospel as preached by Paul. He had been equipped by Paul and was now to become an equipper. He was to entrust what he had learned to "faithful men," which is probably another way of describing the elders of the church. But this task of equipping does not stop with the elders. They also are to become equippers "who will be able to teach others also." The task of raising up new leaders in the church does not belong primarily to Bible colleges or seminaries. It is the task of the elders to identify those young (or not so young) men who will be faithful to carry on the gospel message. Unfortunately, many pastors are either too busy or too insecure to mentor and disciple other gifted men in the church. Thus, this role of the elder is perhaps the most neglected and therefore one that must be emphasized in the local church.

ELDERS AND THE SHARING OF BURDENS

With all the duties elders are required to perform, it is no wonder that in His wisdom God meant for each local church to be led by a plurality of leaders who can share the burden of the ministry. Caring for the church is often too much for one man to handle and can lead to frustration and burnout. Is it any wonder that so many pastorates are short-lived? Many pastors are living and ministering under the incredible burden of shepherding God's people alone. Often there is no one to come beside the pastor and encourage him when he is weary from doing good. From his wisdom, Solomon writes, "Two are better than one, because they have a good reward for their toil. For if they fall, one will lift up his fellow. But woe to him who is alone when he falls and has not another to lift him up! Again, if two lie together, they keep warm, but how can one keep warm alone? And though a man might prevail against one who is alone, two will withstand him—a threefold cord is not quickly broken" (Eccl. 4:9–12). It is difficult for a congregation to become mature and equipped for the work of the ministry through the labor of a single pastor. If one man attempts to do all the work himself, he will begin to neglect other important areas of his life—such as his own spirituality or his own family.

A church is better able to handle cases of church discipline when there is a plurality of elders. A lone pastor will tend to shy away from such confrontation or might be viewed by others as handling the situation too severely. It is usually too much responsibility for a single pastor to carefully handle such a difficult situation. But with the wisdom that comes from a group of godly men, the situation will almost certainly be dealt with in a more God-honoring manner. During this difficult time, the elders can encourage one another to do what is right instead of merely settling with what is expedient. The criticisms that might be leveled against a single pastor do not fall as hard on a group of elders who can shoulder the weight together.

A plurality of elders also provides the church with balance. No one person has all the gifts or the time necessary to provide all that the congregation needs. As a result, most pastors are not capable of adequately fulfilling all the responsibilities set before them. They may be gifted in one area but lacking in another. Some pastors are especially gifted in preaching and teaching. Others are better gifted in administration, counseling, or discipling. By having a team of elders, the deficiencies of one man are balanced by other elders who complement his weaknesses. Thus, it provides a variety of gifts and perspectives that are often absent when one pastor ministers alone. A plurality of elders also allows each elder to focus on his specific calling and gifting instead of expending massive amounts of time and energy on areas of the ministry that he is not particularly gifted in. When the elders function as a team, they will be able to complement each other's weaknesses, allowing each elder to devote most of his time to the area of ministry in which he is most gifted.

Another advantage of having elders is that it better represents the nature of ministry and the church. When the church is led by a single pastor, this conveys the idea that only a select few can serve God in such a capacity. The gulf between the "clergy" and "laity" becomes widened and eventually uncrossable. A plurality of elders, however, demonstrates that doing the work of the ministry is not designated only for a select few. When ordinary members show themselves to be qualified and gifted to serve as elders, it opens a massive door of opportunity for others. They begin to think, "Perhaps some day I can become an elder too." This encourages them to live godly lives so that they too can serve someday as an elder. In this way, plural eldership takes the focus off the paid staff and puts it on the average person, encouraging each person to consider serving in a more committed capacity. Plural eldership gives opportunity for younger leaders to rise up within the congregation because they realize that there is a place for ministry for more than one person in the church.

Christ alone is the head of the church (Col. 1:18). He is the Chief Shepherd, and those whom Christ calls to lead the church are merely undershepherds. They shepherd the congregation under the authority and direction of the Word and the Spirit. But when each local church has only one pastor or senior pastor, this distinction can become blurred. Often, we hear comments like, "I attend Pastor John's church." What people mean by such statements is that they attend the church where Pastor John is the senior pastor. In a sense, this is simply a shortened way to say where they attend church. And yet, such language can lead to a faulty view of the pastoral ministry. The church does not belong to any pastor, and thus it is not really *his* church. Plural eldership, however, tends to keep the focus on Christ as the head of the church.

ELDERS AND EQUALITY

If a plurality of elders is accepted as the appropriate biblical model for today, a question that must be answered relates to the authority that exists among the elders. Should all the elders have the same amount of authority in the church? Or should one (or more) of the elders be given a special authority that weighs heavier than the others? Some contend that the senior pastor should be given more authority because he is the leader of the church. He usually has more pastoral education and training and leads the church on a "full-time" basis. It is argued, therefore, that the "senior pastor" should be granted a special authority that is above the rest of the elders.

All Elders Have Equal Authority

Such a distinction, however, once again creates a separate office and does harm to the unity of the eldership. There are a number of reasons why all the elders should possess equal authority in the church. First, all the elders have to meet the same qualifications. The qualifications do not list certain degrees, and no distinction should be made between teaching elders and ruling elders. Second, all elders share the same responsibilities—primarily teaching and shepherding. Although some may spend more time in these important tasks, all elders will be involved in them to some extent. Also, there should not be a distinction made between elders who serve only part-time and those who serve full-time or between elders who are paid and elders who are unpaid. Third, giving more authority to one elder implicitly creates a separate and distinct office. If the "pastor" (the full-time, paid staff) receives more authority than the "elders" (the part-time, non-staff), the outcome is that an unbiblical distinction has been made. All elders are due the same respect and honor and should be equal in value, power, and rank.

First Among Equals

We would be mistaken, however, to claim that all elders are equal in giftedness or leadership skills. Although all elders share equal authority, not all are equal in experience, dedication, and spiritual gifts. This distinction is often referred to as "first among equals." Jesus himself practiced this concept. Out of the twelve disciples, Peter, James, and John were chosen to receive special attention from their Master. And out of the three, Peter was often singled out and given special leadership. Because of his gifts and calling, he was the most prominent among the apostles. Yet, Peter was an apostle just like the rest of the Twelve. He was never given a special title. He did not wear different clothes or receive a higher salary. The others were not subordinate to him and did not function as his attendants or servants. He was equal in rank and authority to the rest of the apostles. At the same time, however, he was a natural leader and as such became the "first among equals." This concept also is illustrated in the relationship of Philip and Stephen among the Seven and in the relationship between Paul and Barnabas (Acts 6:8; 13:13; 14:12).

The "first among equals" concept is also expressed in the way congregations are to honor their elders. Paul writes, "Let the elders who rule well be considered worthy of double honor, especially those who labor in preaching and teaching" (1 Tim. 5:17). Thus, special honor and respect (and pay) is to be given to those who prove themselves faithful and effective in their ministry, especially in the areas of communicating God's holy Word. We know from the qualifications listed in 1 Timothy 3 that all elders must be "able to teach" (v. 2). Some, however, may be especially gifted in preaching or teaching. Because of their training and giftedness, they may be asked to preach more often than the others. They do not need a special title in front of their names if they are employed by the church and have dedicated their lives to "full-time" ministry. Thus, the principle of "first among equals" allows for elders to have different functions based on giftedness without creating a separate or distinct office of one who is superior to the rest of the elders.

The Benefits of "First Among Equals"

The benefits of this principle are immediately evident. First, it allows those who are especially called and gifted to dedicate more of their time to the pastoral ministry. Those elders who have other full-time employment are, of course, extremely important to the ministry and can be greatly used by God. Paul himself was a tentmaker and often worked this trade to support his ministry. But in today's society, an elder who works a full-time job often has little time or energy to devote to the church. Sometimes it is more beneficial to the life and growth of the church if an elder is employed by the church. As a result, he is able to dedicate all his energy to the study and proclamation of God's Word, to shepherding, to counseling, or to other important tasks.

A second benefit is that those who are exceptionally gifted as leaders or teachers have accountability. They are not given a higher position as full-time workers but are simply given a greater responsibility. They are allowed to exercise their gifts to the fullest without being given unmatched authority in the church. Thus, this structure provides the needed accountability. The danger is—and far too often it is the case—that the other elders will neglect their duties and turn over the care of the church to one or two elders who are on the church's payroll. Another danger is that one elder will abuse the principle of "first among equals" by claiming that his higher calling and greater gifts must mean that he is granted a higher position in the church. But simply because one elder may have greater influence does not mean that he holds a higher office. It would be unwise to grant one elder more formal authority than the others.

The Challenges of "First Among Equals"
The "first among equals" principle must be exercised with great care. It is important for the "first" among the elders to understand his role. If he seeks to take advantage of his prominence in a way that elevates himself, biblical eldership will not function properly. As the elder who is the most visible because of his teaching and preaching responsibilities,

he will be able to influence the congregation in ways the other elders cannot. Thus, he must consciously and deliberately seek to build up the other elders so that they will be just as respected by the congregation. Because he is one of the elders, he is accountable to the other elders and therefore must be willing to defer to them.

The "nonprofessional" elders also face challenges. They must learn to view themselves as full-fledged shepherds who are responsible for the members of the congregation. Simply because they are not "full-time" elders does not mean that they have less authority than those who are fully paid by the church. Being an elder also requires great sacrifice. The task of shepherding involves much time and energy and is often burdensome (see 2 Cor. 11:28, where Paul speaks of the daily pressure he bears from the churches he planted). In addition, these elders must be willing to keep the "first among equals" accountable. This means that elders must not be afraid of confrontation.

ELDERS AND ACCOUNTABILITY

If having a plurality of elders that share equal authority is God's design, there will be many benefits to be gained by following God's wisdom. Although having a plurality of elders does not guarantee the church leadership will not encounter problems or conflict, it does at least provide several safeguards against some problems and difficulties that a single-pastor church often faces—especially in the area of biblical accountability.

Biblical accountability is needed for two reasons. First, it helps protect a pastor from error. Pastors often possess a lot of authority in their churches—too much authority with too little accountability. Such authority can cause one to believe that he is more important than others and thus to become proud. Others may act in ways that are insensitive or unscriptural but be blinded to their faults. Each person has certain blind spots and faults or deficiencies that can distort one's judgment. If a pastor has little or no accountability, these tendencies can go unchecked. When a church has only one pastor, or a senior pastor with unmatched power, there is usually no accountability structure built in to the system—except for the congregation or the deacons to fire the pastor, which is far too common.

A plural eldership model helps to provide the needed accountability that is lacking in most churches so that one man does not dominate the church. There must be others who are equal in status and authority who can face a fellow elder and confront him if he is being unreasonable or is living in sin—just as Peter was confronted by Paul (a fellow apostle) when Peter refused to eat with Gentiles (Gal. 2:11–14). A pastor needs the constant reminder that he is not above the law but is subject to the other elders. Every pastor is prone to sin and must constantly be monitoring his spiritual walk. Paul warns the Ephesian elders, "Pay careful attention to yourselves and to all the flock" (Acts 20:28). Later he exhorts Timothy, "Keep a close watch on yourself and on the teaching" (1 Tim. 4:16). But a pastor not only needs to keep watch over his own life; he also needs the help of others.

Second, biblical accountability is needed to help foster maturity and godliness among the elders. The author of Hebrews warns, "Take care, brothers, lest there be in any of you an evil, unbelieving heart, leading you to fall away from the living God. But exhort one another every day, as long as it is called 'today,' that none of you may be hardened by the deceitfulness of sin" (Heb. 3:12–13). As the elders serve and lead together, they will often be challenged by the godly examples they see in each other so that they hold their confession "firm to the end" (Heb. 3:14). They will "stir up one another to love and good works" (Heb. 10:24). The more mature elders can help train the younger ones in how to be effective shepherds. As the proverb says, "Iron sharpens iron, and one man sharpens another" (Prov. 27:17).

CONCLUSION

Every church should have elders because pastors need help and accountability. They need help because the duties of a pastor are extremely important and at times overwhelming. Among other things, the work of a pastor involves leading, shepherding, teaching, and equipping. This work is too difficult to do alone. Without help from properly qualified and gifted men who can share in this important work, a lone pastor will be crushed by the weight of ministry. God's design is that a group of leaders share this burden together. This helps prevent pastoral burnout and allows pastors to serve with increased joy. It also provides the church balance by offering a variety of perspectives and gifts. Every Christian has certain gifts, but no Christian is gifted in every area. Having a plurality of elders adds a fullness and balance to the leadership of the church.

In addition, elders provide needed accountability. For this accountability to be real and effective, all the elders/pastors must possess equal authority. It is dangerous to give more authority to those who appear to possess greater leadership and teaching gifts. In fact, it is precisely because they have greater gifts that they need greater accountability. Many pastors have too much authority and too little accountability (some may have no authority and/or no accountability). Biblical accountability protects the character and witness of elders and fosters maturity and godliness among them as they challenge each other toward love and good deeds.

Chapter 3

It Produces a Healthier Church

A third reason every church should have elders is that this system of church government provides the fertile soil for the church to grow and bear much fruit. Although many churches have abandoned or ignored this model, the long-term effect has been to weaken the church. Having qualified elders provides stability to a church and keeps a church from relying solely on professionals to do the work of the ministry. By having unpaid/non-staff elders, the church also is able to have more leaders, who can then help lead the church.

ELDERS AND HISTORY

With the many benefits of plural eldership, one might get the impression that most churches embrace this teaching. Unfortunately, this is not the case. This does not mean that there are not churches that embrace and practice plural eldership. Numerous churches and denominations have diligently applied the teaching of Scripture to their system of church government. In addition, there are hundreds of church leaders who are seeking to restore a more biblical form of eldership to their churches. When they read what the New Testament has to say concerning church organization and leadership, they ask themselves, "Why doesn't my church look like this?" They read of Paul appointing elders in churches and of elders mentioned in his epistles and ask, "Why doesn't my church have elders?" But the fact remains that having a plurality of elders is a foreign concept in most evangelical churches. This was not always the case. In generations past, many churches were led by elders. But over the years this model of church polity began to fade into history. Why was this the case? Let me offer three reasons why so few churches have a plurality of elders today.

Lack of Qualified Men

In order to be qualified to be an elder, a man must meet certain qualifications (1 Tim. 3:1–7; Titus 1:6–9; 1 Peter 5:2–3). Although most of these qualifications are what is expected of all Christians, very few men actually meet the qualifications. Of course, the qualifications can be applied too rigorously so that almost no one can meet them. Godliness, not perfection, is the requirement. Yet, even when the requirements are fairly applied, there seems to be so few who are left to serve. It seems that the desire to serve as an elder has all but vanished in the church. Men are so preoccupied in advancing their careers that the church is virtually ignored and with it the spirituality required to serve as an elder. Paul says that it is a "noble task" for a man to aspire to the office of elder (1 Tim. 3:1). Spiritual laziness and a zeal for the

American dream have squelched the desire of potential elders. For many, it is simply easier to hire someone from the outside to handle the "business" of the church. We have become a service-oriented society. When we need something done, we simply hire someone to do it. Unfortunately, this mentality has carried over into the church. The pastorate has become so professionalized that many congregations will not even consider hiring a person as their pastor unless he has a "Dr." in front of his name. As a result, many churches that began with the hope of having a plurality of elders simply gave up and opted for the more conventional (though less biblical) model of having one pastor and a board of deacons.

Lack of Biblical Knowledge

It is a simple fact that in today's churches the average Christian has never been taught the doctrine of a plurality of elders. Most pastors don't bother themselves with such "irrelevant" issues such as church government, so they never teach their people what the Bible says about it. Proper church government, however, is far from being irrelevant. Many churches have become so pragmatic that they simply use whatever model of leadership seems to be successful in the marketplace. They claim that the Bible does not give us a specific leadership model but allows flexibility for each church to "do what is right in its own eyes." Consequently, the doctrine of biblical eldership has fallen on rocky soil and is devoured by the birds before it ever enters the heart of the church and bears fruit.

Fear of Change

Fear is a motivating factor in the lives of many people and the fear of change often is what holds back a church from adopting and implementing plural eldership. Pastors fear that the congregation will reject their ideas. They fear that the church will split if they try to change the constitution or bylaws in regard to church government. They fear that their efforts will fail and the church will be worse off than before. They fear having to do the hard work of educating the congregation about eldership. Other pastors fear that they might lose some of their power and authority in the church.

Those in the congregation also are fearful. They fear that things might not be as comfortable as they now are. They fear that elders will take authority away from the congregation. They fear that they might lose their right to vote in business meetings. They fear that their church might be adopting the church government of a denomination different from their own. They fear that they might be expected to lead. They fear that they might be asked to stop leading.

But often what people fear the most is simply change. They may even acknowledge that such a doctrine is found in the Bible, but they are not convinced that it is worth the trouble of actually conforming their church polity to the Scriptures. Pastors often talk about the need for changing their church government but never take any steps to actually do anything about it. Fear has become a powerful deterrent to recovering biblical eldership. The Bible, however, tells us that "perfect love casts out fear" (1 John 4:18).

For many years churches have been looking to the corporate world for successful models of leadership. In order for the church to be successful, they say, the pastor needs to function like a CEO. He needs to be a strong leader and a visionary. He must speak to the needs of the people and at the same time tell them what they want to hear. Congregations that have followed through with this model often look more like corporations than churches. The end result often leaves many people dissatisfied and spiritually malnourished. As a result, there is a growing desire for churches to organize themselves according to the wisdom of God and not the wisdom of man. "For the foolishness of God is wiser than men, and the weakness of God is stronger than men" (1 Cor. 1:25). As churches grow in their commitment to God and to His Word, they will become more concerned with the leadership structure of their churches. Men will desire to live godly lives to the glory of God and will be qualified to serve in His church. Pastors will become convicted and begin to teach the congregation about biblical church polity. And fear will disappear as the truth of God's Word emboldens elders and their congregations to live and minister according to God's design for the church.

ELDERS AND QUALIFICATIONS

Having elders does not guarantee a healthy church, but it does enable it. But what exactly are the qualifications for someone to serve as an elder? Must he be paid by the church? Must he serve "full-time"? Must he be formally trained?

The qualifications for elders/overseers are found in 1 Timothy 3:1–7 and Titus 1:5–9. When reading the qualifications for an elder or overseer, one is immediately struck by the relative simplicity of the qualifications. In fact, the qualifications for an elder are the basic characteristics that are expected of all Christians. The only exceptions are that an elder must not be a recent convert and must be able to teach. The focus of the qualifications is on who a person is more than what a person does. That is, the focus is on the character of the person, not his gifts or personality. The following chart provides a comparison of the qualifications found in 1 Timothy 3 with those in Titus 1. The qualifications in Titus 1 are rearranged to match the order given in 1 Timothy 3. Those qualifications found only in one list are italicized.

1 Timothy 3	Titus 1
above reproach	above reproach
the husband of one wife	the husband of one wife
sober-minded	
self-controlled	self-controlled
respectable	
hospitable	hospitable
able to teach	hold firm to the trustworthy word as taught—give instruction in sound doctrine and also rebuke those who contradict it
not a drunkard	not a drunkard
not violent	not violent
gentle	
not quarrelsome	
not a lover of money	not greedy for gain
manage his own household well, keeping his children submissive	his children are believers and not open to the charge of debauchery or insubordination
not a recent convert	
well thought of by outsiders	
	not arrogant
	not quick-tempered
	a lover of good
	upright
	holy
	disciplined

For the most part, the qualifications given seem to be listed in random order. The one exception is that both lists begin with the qualifications of being "above reproach" and "the husband of one wife" (1 Tim. 3:2; Titus 1:6). These requirements can be divided into situational, family, and moral qualifications.

Situational Qualifications

These qualifications relate to one's situation in life. They are not really moral or spiritual qualifications but rather reveal one's desire and ability to serve. They also relate to the time of one's conversion and how non-Christians view the genuineness of that conversion.

- *Desire to serve* (1 Tim. 3:1). Although not formally a qualification, Paul mentions that it is a good thing ("a noble task") for someone to aspire to the office of overseer. "Noble" is translated from the Greek word *kalos,* which means "good," "excellent," or "worthwhile." While it is possible some may desire this office from impure motives such as greed or pride, Paul wants to make clear that those who are chosen to serve should want to serve. Churches often nominate people to service and then have to twist their arms to get them to reluctantly accept the position. These people may serve faithfully, but they seldom really experience joy and fulfillment in their service. It is better to select those people who are eager to serve. Indeed, it is best to select those people who are already joyfully serving in some capacity, although they may have no formal office in the church. Those who desire to serve God as elders desire a good thing. But desire alone is never enough. This desire must be accompanied by moral character and spiritual capability.

- *Able to teach* (1 Tim. 3:2; Titus 1:9). This is the only qualification that directly relates to an elder's duties in the church (although 1 Tim. 3:4–5 speaks of managing and caring for the church). Elders must be able to communicate God's Word in a way that is accurate and understandable. In Titus, Paul expands on what he wrote in 1 Timothy. He adds that an overseer "must hold firm to the trustworthy word as taught, so that he may be able to give instruction in sound doctrine and also to rebuke those who contradict it" (Titus 1:9). An elder must not only be "able to teach," but he must also teach sound doctrine and correct those who are in error. He cannot have merely a cursory knowledge of the Bible; he must be immersed in the teachings of Scripture so that he can both exhort in sound doctrine and rebuke those who reject sound doctrine.

  If all elders must be "able to teach," does that mean that all elders must teach or preach publicly? Such an interpretation is probably more restrictive than what Paul has in mind. Certainly, all elders should be involved in some kind of teaching. It would seem odd for Paul to require that all elders be able to teach if some of them are not involved in any type of teaching ministry. All elders must be able to teach and should be using their teaching abilities or gifts actively in the church. But the type of teaching should not be limited to preaching on Sunday mornings or at other times when the entire congregation is gathered. Some elders may not be gifted in teaching or preaching to large groups but may have an incredible gift to teach or disciple in a small group setting.

- *Not a recent convert* (1 Tim. 3:6). In 1 Timothy, Paul writes that an elder must not be a new believer. He then gives the reason for this qualification: "or he may become puffed up with conceit and fall into the condemnation of the devil" (1 Tim. 3:6). When a recent convert takes on an important and respected leadership role without the deep maturity that comes with time, he may become filled with pride and end up ruining his ministry and defaming the name of God. A new convert does not truly understand his own weaknesses and the temptations that might ensnare him. As a result, he is more vulnerable to pride, which will lead to his destruction (Prov. 16:18). Time is therefore needed to let the new believer mature in his faith and gain the respect of others through faithful service in lesser roles. The difficulty is that Paul does not specify what constitutes a "recent convert." Was he referring to six months, one year, or ten years? Perhaps the answer to this question depends on the congregation or historical circumstances involved. In some churches, it might be unwise to let a person become an elder who has been a Christian for only five years. In other churches, however, it may be unwise to wait that long.

- *Well thought of by outsiders* (1 Tim. 3:7). "Outsiders," or non-Christians, often seem to be better judges of character than those in the church.

Neighbors, coworkers, or relatives actually may spend much more time with the person than does his fellow church members. An elder must maintain a good reputation before a world of watching unbelievers. If the church allows a person who has a bad reputation with non-Christians to become an elder, the unbelievers will scoff and mock the church for being hypocrites. A man who is unfaithful to his family, dishonest in his business, or rude to his neighbors will bring shame on himself, the church, and ultimately the gospel. Paul warns that those who have a sinful or unfavorable reputation with outsiders can "fall into disgrace, into a snare of the devil" (1 Tim. 3:7). The world is waiting to point their finger and criticize and disgrace the church. Consequently, the devil will use one's bad reputation to ensnare the person deeper into sin. Thus, an elder must have a good reputation with non-Christians.

Family Qualifications

The second area of qualifications relates to the family life of the candidate. He must be faithful to his wife and manage his children well before he can be considered fit to lead the church of God.

- *The husband of one wife* (1 Tim. 3:2; Titus 1:6). This qualification appears at the forefront of both lists, directly after the general qualification of being "above reproach." This placement suggests the importance of marital and sexual faithfulness and also highlights that this may have been a problem in the Ephesian and Cretean churches. The best interpretation of this difficult phrase is to understand it as referring to the faithfulness of a husband toward his wife. He must be a "one-woman man." That is, there must be no other woman in his life to whom he relates emotionally or physically. It is important for men to put a hedge of protection around their lives so that they do not get into a position where they become emotionally or physically connected with another woman. As a general rule, it is best if a man is never alone with a woman who is not his wife. Unfortunately, many men have disqualified themselves from ministry because of unwise decisions regarding their contact with other women. The Bible is full of warnings about sexual unfaithfulness, but these warnings often go unheeded.

- *Manage his own household well* (1 Tim. 3:4–5; Titus 1:6). The second family qualification relates to the man's role as father. Paul writes, "He must manage his own household well, with all dignity keeping his children submissive" (1 Tim. 3:4). An elder must have respectful, obedient children. He must not be heavy-handed and authoritarian with his children but must deal with them "with all dignity." A godly father does not seek to crush the spirit of his children, forcing them into submission by harsh discipline. Rather, he relates to them with dignity and seeks to nurture their hearts. Paul writes, "Fathers, do not provoke your children to anger, but bring them up in the discipline and instruction of the Lord" (Eph. 6:4).

Paul then gives the reason why this qualification is important: "For if someone does not know how to manage his own household, how will he care for God's church?" (1 Tim. 3:5). Paul makes an important parallel between the family and the church. If a man is not able to lead his family so that his children are generally respectful and obedient, then he is not fit to lead the church, the family of God. The leadership of his family becomes tangible proof that he is either fit or unfit to lead in God's church. In addition, by neglecting his family—even for the sake of "the ministry"—a man can become disqualified to serve as an elder. Family life must take precedence over the ministry: God first, family second, ministry third.

In Paul's letter to Titus, he states that an elder's children must be "believers and not open to the charge of debauchery or insubordination" (Titus 1:6). The word translated "believers" (*pistos*) is better translated "faithful" in this context (see HCSB, KJV, NKJV). This interpretation is confirmed by the fact that 1 Timothy 3 does not mention the need for elders' children to be believers. Furthermore, the following phrase in Titus 1 clarifies what Paul meant by "faithful," when he states that they must not be open to the charge of debauchery or insubordination. Thus, an elder's children must be respectful and obedient but not necessarily believers since that is not something an elder can control (though he can certainly influence it).

Moral Qualifications

In 1 Timothy 3 and Titus 1 Paul lists several moral qualifications for elders. We will first consider those characteristics elders are to model and then discuss those characteristics elders are to avoid.

- *Above reproach* (1 Tim. 3:2; Titus 1:6). The general or overarching qualification for an elder is that he must be "above reproach." This requirement does not call for perfection but for godliness. To be above reproach means to be free from any blemishes of character or conduct. His relationship with his wife and children is commendable and he has no glaring moral weaknesses. Outsiders cannot point their finger and discredit his profession to be a faithful follower of Christ.

- *Sober-minded* (1 Tim. 3:2). This word is sometimes translated "temperate" and is often used in connection with sobriety from alcohol (wine). In the context of 1 Timothy 3, however, it is best understood as referring to mental sobriety; that is, a mind that can think clearly and spiritually about important matters. It is the ability to be self-controlled, having a balanced judgment and being able to rationally make coolheaded decisions. Elders must be mentally and emotionally stable enough to make important decisions in the midst of problems and pressures they will face in their ministry.

- *Self-controlled* (1 Tim. 3:2; Titus 1:8). Similar to the previous qualification, this characteristic refers to the need for disciplined exercise of good judgment. It speaks of being prudent, sound-minded, and discreet. Such discretion often is needed by elders, who constantly have to make difficult decisions in the face of problems and disagreements.

- *Respectable* (1 Tim. 3:2). An elder also must have

character that is respectable. It is not enough to get his respect from his office. If others are to follow and emulate him, he must prove that his life is worth following. His character therefore must be well balanced and virtuous if he is to be respected.

• *Hospitable* (1 Tim. 3:2; Titus 1:8). An elder's life must be open so that others can be a part of it. Being hospitable means making time not only for one's family, but also for others. The theme of hospitality is an important biblical virtue (see Job 31:32; Rom. 12:13; Heb. 13:21; 1 Peter 4:9). If an elder is to get to know people and invest in their lives, he must take the time to build relationships with them. If he is to effectively shepherd the flock of God, his home must be open so that he can minister to them more than just on Sunday mornings.

• *Gentle* (1 Tim. 3:3). The word translated "gentle" also can mean "kind," "gracious," or "forbearing." In Philippians 4:5, Paul writes, "Let your gentleness be made known to all" (my translation). A gentle person is not overbearing but patient with others, especially when they have done wrong. He does not retaliate when wronged but returns love for evil.

• *A lover of good* (Titus 1:8). This characteristic is closely related to hospitality. It involves willingly helping others and seeking their good.

• *Upright* (Titus 1:8). The Greek word *dikaios* means "just" or "righteous." To be upright or righteous means living according to God's Word. First John

3:7 states, "Whoever practices righteousness is righteous, as he is righteous." Elders must abide by God's righteous standard revealed in His Word. An elder who is righteous will make fair, just, and upright decisions for the church. Job is described as a man who was "blameless and upright, one who feared God and turned away from evil" (Job 1:1).

+ *Holy* (Titus 1:8). Sometimes translated "devout," this characteristic involves being wholly devoted to God and His Word. It entails being set apart to God in order to obey His will. A holy person is dedicated to glorifying the name of God regardless of what others may think.

+ *Disciplined* (Titus 1:8). Similar to the qualification of being "self-controlled," this characteristic involves self-discipline in every aspect of one's life, including physical desires. An undisciplined person yields easily to temptation, but a disciplined person fights against lust, anger, laziness, and other ungodly traits. Shepherding God's people is hard work, and discipline is needed to fulfill this ministry faithfully and effectively.

+ *Not a drunkard* (1 Tim. 3:3; Titus 1:7). A man is disqualified for the office of elder if he is a drunkard (addicted to wine or other strong drink). Such a person lacks self-control and is undisciplined. The abuse of alcohol is a problem in most cultures and often results in ruined lives, marriages, and ministries. Notice, however, that Paul does not say that it is wrong to drink alcohol. Rather, he is referring to the excesses of drinking too much alcohol and drinking it too often. As a matter of fact, he later tells Timothy to drink a little wine for his stomach problems (1 Tim. 5:23). Although many churches require not only their leadership but all members as well to abstain from alcohol, this requirement is nowhere found in Scripture. The real issue is the abuse of any substance that would bring shame on the person and reproach on the church.

- *Not violent* (1 Tim. 3:3; Titus 1:7). A person who is "violent," or "pugnacious," as it is sometimes translated, is one who is easily irritated and has a bad temper. Such a person is often ready to fight rather than to calmly talk through a difficult situation. A violent man not only uses verbal abuse but also is ready to physically assault those who anger him. On the contrary, an elder must be self-controlled and patient, willing to turn the other cheek when wronged. He must be able to calmly and rationally deal with heated arguments and tense situations that often find their way into the church.

- *Not quarrelsome* (1 Tim. 3:3). A man who is not quarrelsome is gentle and peaceful. People are constantly quarreling, even in the church. There are quarrels over doctrine, quarrels over the color of the carpet in the sanctuary, and quarrels over whether the church should sing hymns or choruses. An elder, however, must be able to deal with these tensions and not add to them. He must be a peacemaker and find a way to bring about reconciliation. If he is quarrelsome himself, he will not be able to effectively lead and may even divide the congregation. As Paul later writes, "The Lord's servant must not be quarrelsome but kind to everyone, able to teach, patiently enduring evil, correcting his opponents with gentleness" (2 Tim. 2:24–25). Paul also reminds Titus to encourage the congregation "to speak evil of no one, to avoid quarreling, to be gentle, and to show perfect courtesy toward all people" (Titus 3:2).

• *Not a lover of money* (1 Tim. 3:3; Titus 1:7). The love of money is a serious problem in the church. It was in Paul's day, and it is in ours. Paul writes, "Those who desire to be rich fall into temptation, into a snare, into many senseless and harmful desires that plunge people into ruin and destruction" (1 Tim. 6:9). The results of loving money can end in the destruction of one's soul. This is no small sin. Paul continues, "For the love of money is a root of all kinds of evils. It is through this craving that some have wandered away from the faith and pierced themselves with many pangs" (1 Tim. 6:10). The Bible is full of warnings to the rich. Jesus Himself said, "It is easier for a camel to go through the eye of a needle than for a rich person to enter the kingdom of God" (Mark 10:25). Consequently, it is not difficult to understand why Paul includes this qualification in both 1 Timothy and Titus.

If a person is a lover of money, it is difficult for him also to be a lover of God. If our passions are divided we become ineffective and distracted. Money itself is not the problem, however. It is the *love* of money. Whether we are considered rich and have plenty of money or are poor, the issue at stake is where our desires are found. It is not those who *are* rich who fall into temptation but those who *desire* to be rich.

Paul's wording for the qualification in Titus is different than that in 1 Timothy. He states that an elder must not be "greedy for gain" (Titus 1:7). A greedy person is never content with God's provision but is constantly seeking ways to acquire more money—often in ways that are immoral and unethical. In 2 Corinthians, Paul warns of some ministers who peddle the Word of God for money (2 Cor. 2:17; cf. Titus 1:11). Likewise, Peter states that elders must shepherd the flock of God "not for shameful gain" (1 Peter 5:2).

Elders should be those who are free from the love and controlling influence of money. A pastor should not have unchecked control over the funds of a church. The elders must be accountable to one another and to the congregation as a whole. How many times have leaders fallen due to unethical practices with the church's finances? In contrast, we must heed the Word of God, which states, "Keep your life free from love of money, and be content with what you have, for he has said, 'I will never leave you nor forsake you'" (Heb. 13:5).

• *Not arrogant* (Titus 1:7). An arrogant person is a self-willed person, one who is constantly insisting that things be done his way. This is the opposite of being "gentle" or "forbearing" (1 Tim. 3:3). One who is arrogant is inconsiderate of other people's opinions and feelings and attempts to get what he wants regardless of the cost to others. Such a person does not make a good elder because the elders must work together as a team, seeking the best for others and not for themselves. A shepherd must be gentle with the sheep and not seek to overpower them by his strong will.

- *Not quick-tempered* (Titus 1:7). David tells us that God is "merciful and gracious, slow to anger and abounding in steadfast love" (Ps. 103:8). Those who lead the church are to model the characteristics of their heavenly Father and be slow to anger. A quick-tempered man, however, is not only easily angered, but he is also unable to control that anger. He quickly lashes out at others, rather than displaying the patience and self-control of Christ. Although all anger is not sin (Paul tells us, "Be angry and do not sin," Eph. 4:26; cf. Ps. 4:4), James reminds us that "the anger of man does not produce the righteousness that God requires" (James 1:20). Furthermore, "A man of wrath stirs up strife, and one given to anger causes much transgression" (Prov. 29:22). An elder must be able to deal with difficult and emotionally charged situations that arise in one's personal life and in the context of the church.

Is There a Minimum Age for an Elder?

Neither the Old Testament nor the New Testament specifies the minimum age of an elder. In Jewish culture, a man became an elder based on his moral authority derived from his age, heredity, experience, knowledge, or wealth. It was not an official position that was given to him by someone higher in authority but was a title of honor and respect that he received from the people of his community. Of course, one's age was a prominent factor in whether a man was worthy to be counted among the "elders." In its basic meaning, the term *elder* refers to someone who has entered old age. It would be wrong, however, to conclude that all elders were technically considered to have entered old age (usually considered to be sixty).

In the early Christian church, those who were given certain leadership positions also were known as "elders." Because the term for elder is often translated "older man" (1 Tim. 5:1; Titus 2:2), many assume that only old men can serve as elders. Yet, an elder in the Christian church does not have to be a senior citizen. We are told that an elder must not be a new convert (1 Tim. 3:6), but nowhere does Paul specify that an elder must be a certain age. In contrast, when listing the qualification for widows to receive financial support from the church, Paul indicates that she must be sixty years of age (1 Tim. 5:9).

When Paul wrote 1 and 2 Timothy, Timothy was probably about thirty-five years old. He was approximately twenty years old when he joined Paul's ministry team during his second missionary trip, which was about fifteen years before the letters to him were written. We know that Timothy was still considered young when Paul wrote to him because he says, "Let no one despise you for your youth" (1 Tim. 4:12). Later Paul warns Timothy to "flee youthful passions" (2 Tim. 2:22). If Timothy, who held a position as Paul's apostolic delegate with the authority to appoint elders, was still considered "young," then it would seem unwise to limit the office of elder to those who are considered "old." The key issues are: (1) Is the person spiritually mature, meeting the specified qualifications, and (2) will the congregation respect his leadership? In some younger congregations, a man thirty years old might be well respected, whereas in an older congregation, a man forty years old might be considered quite young. Age alone does not guarantee spirituality. Those who are selected must be mature, wise, and respected by those they will serve.

The qualifications for an elder are the basic characteristics that are expected of all believers. Elders are not super-spiritual people but are those who are mature in their faith and live consistent, humble lives. An elder has a healthy and pure relationship with his wife, and he is a godly leader in his home. His character has no glaring blemishes, and his godliness is even recognized by those who are not Christians. He is not perfect, but his life is characterized by integrity.

ELDERS AND AFFORDABILITY

Many churches struggle to adequately pay their pastor(s). As the church grows, the pastor is given more and more responsibility but is given little or no additional help. Often the bottom line is simply that the church cannot afford to hire another pastor. However, the idea that only full-time, paid pastors can lead the church is not found in the Scriptures. Such a view can lead to an unhealthy church. Having both paid/staff and unpaid/non-staff elders allows for a church to have more leaders than a comparable church with only paid elders/pastors. According to the Bible, there is no requirement that an elder must be paid to be an elder. And yet, it is the responsibility of the church to pay an elder for his work if he needs to be financially supported.

The Right of Elders to Be Paid

Besides being a missionary who traveled extensively planting churches, Paul also worked a "secular" job. Luke records that when Paul came to Corinth during his second missionary journey, he stayed with Aquila and Priscilla because they were of the same trade as the apostle (i.e., they were both tentmakers; Acts 18:3). As a general rule, Paul did not receive money from the people to whom he was currently ministering. In 1 Corinthians 9:1–18, Paul uses the example of his not accepting money from the Corinthians in order to illustrate how he willingly relinquished his rights. Thus, in 1 Corinthians 9, Paul offers several reasons why he is entitled to receive financial compensation for his labor among the Corinthians. His point, however, is that although he had the right to receive such compensation, he refused any support so that the gospel would not be hindered. In support of his right to compensation, Paul not only offers arguments from culture (1 Cor. 9:7) but also bolsters his position by quoting the Old Testament. He states,

> Do I say these things on human authority? Does not the Law say the same? For it is written in the Law of Moses, "You shall not muzzle an ox when it treads out the grain." Is it for oxen that God is concerned? Does he not speak entirely for our sake? It was written for our sake." (1 Cor. 9:8–10)

In this text, Paul quotes from Deuteronomy 25:4, "You shall not muzzle an ox when it is treading out the grain." The oxen doing the work were not to be muzzled but were to have freedom to eat the grain below them. The obvious point of this verse is that it would be cruel to deny those doing the work the fruit of their labor. Paul is using the common rabbinical argument of lesser to the greater. In other words, if animals that work are not to be denied reward for their labor, how much more should men be granted payment for their labor. Paul simply applies this principle to himself and his ministry among the Corinthians. Just as it is wrong to muzzle an ox while he is threshing (i.e., working), so also it is wrong not to support financially those who work in order to advance the kingdom of God. He later supports this principle by appealing to the words of the Lord: "In the same way, the Lord commanded that those who proclaim the gospel should get their living by the gospel" (1 Cor. 9:14).

Paul believed not only that he had the right to receive financial compensation for his labors, but that hardworking elders had claim to that right as well. In his first letter to Timothy he writes, "Let the elders who rule well be considered worthy of double honor, especially those who labor in preaching and teaching" (1 Tim. 5:17). Although the normal meaning of the word translated "honor," refers to the respect or worth given to someone, in this context it clearly includes the idea of financial support. In 1 Timothy 5:3, Paul commands the church, "Honor widows who are truly widows," which clearly refers to financial support (see esp. vv. 4, 8, 16). Furthermore, in 1 Timothy 5:18 Paul quotes Deuteronomy 25:4 ("You shall not muzzle an ox when it treads out the grain") and a saying of Jesus ("The laborer deserves his wages," Matt. 10:10; Luke 10:7) to confirm that financial support is in view. Elders who spend their days shepherding and teaching the church not only should be respected for their duties but also should be financially compensated (also see Gal. 6:6).

The Right of Elders Not to Be Paid

In the previous section we established the biblical truth that elders who spend most of their time teaching and shepherding the congregation deserve to be paid. However, this does not mean that all (or any) of the elders must be paid for their work or that only those who work full-time for the church can rightfully be called "elders," or "pastors." As an apostle and missionary, Paul certainly had the right to be supported by the churches he established and in which he labored. But for the sake of the gospel, he chose not to claim this right.

Just like Paul, there are many elders who are self-supported in the sense that they draw a salary from outside the church. They spend much of their free time in helping to shepherd the congregation, but they are not paid for their labors. Some churches have difficulty financially supporting one or more elders. By having elders who do not receive monetary compensation for their work, the church is able to include more men as elders without the extra burden of supporting them financially. This situation allows the elders to shepherd the congregation more effectively.

CONCLUSION

In the last century, many churches have abandoned the concept of an elder-led church for a more convenient— though less biblical and less efficient—model. Having a plurality of elders, including unpaid/non-staff elders, makes for a healthier church by providing godly leadership for the church. It is unfortunate that many churches virtually ignore the untapped wisdom of godly men in the congregation. Including non-staff elders in the leadership of the church also provides stability to the church. If a church relies solely on hired, professional pastors to lead the church, there is often panic and confusion when that pastor decides to leave for another church. A church that has unpaid/non-staff elders inevitably will have a different experience because there will always be leaders in the church capable of preaching and teaching the congregation. Thus, the church will become less dependent on paid staff.

But often the qualifications for elders are simply ignored or are incorrectly interpreted and applied. Nowhere does the

Bible state that elders must serve full-time or be formally/ seminary trained. The qualifications given in Scripture focus on one's maturity and moral character. Neither does the Bible state that elders must be paid—although those who give most of their time and energy to shepherding and teaching the congregation should be compensated. Those elders who do not work "full-time" for the church or who are not "staff" should not be viewed as having less authority than those who are officially employed by the church. Non-staff elders provide support for the other elders in helping to shepherd the congregation without the added burden on the congregation of supporting them financially.

Chapter 4

It Promotes the Biblical Role of Deacons

A final reason every church should have elders is because elders are uniquely given the task of shepherding,
leading, and teaching the congregation. This is not the duty
of deacons. The biblical role of deacons is to take care of the
physical and logistical needs of the church so that the elders
can concentrate on their primary calling.

THE BACKGROUND OF DEACONS
"Deacon" is a translation of the Greek term *diakonos*,
which normally means "servant." Only context can determine
whether the term is being used in its ordinary sense or as the
technical designation of a church officer. The Greek term is
used twenty-nine times in the New Testament, but only three
or four of those occurrences refer to an officeholder (Rom.

16:1[?]; Phil. 1:1; 1 Tim. 3:8, 12). Whereas there are some parallels between the Jewish elder and the Christian elder, there does not seem to be a parallel to the role of deacon in Jewish or Greek society.

The origin of the deacon is not known for certain, but many scholars believe that the Seven chosen in Acts 6 provide the prototype of the New Testament deacon. The reason many are hesitant to call the Seven the first "deacons" is because the noun *diakonos* ("deacon") does not occur in the text. Only the related verb *diakoneō* ("to serve") is found (Acts 6:2). Another dissimilarity is that the text mentions the apostles but not elders. Therefore, a direct correlation is difficult to make. Still, Acts 6 does provide a pattern or paradigm that seems to have been continued in the early church. It is necessary, then, to investigate this passage in more detail.

> Now in these days when the disciples were increasing in number, a complaint by the Hellenists arose against the Hebrews because their widows were being neglected in the daily distribution. And the twelve summoned the full number of the disciples and said, "It is not right that we should give up preaching the word of God to serve tables. Therefore, brothers, pick out from among you seven men of good repute, full of the Spirit and of wisdom, whom we will appoint to this duty. But we will devote ourselves to prayer and to the ministry of the word." And what they said pleased the whole gathering, and they chose Stephen, a man full of faith and of the Holy Spirit, and Philip, and Prochorus, and Nicanor, and Timon, and Parmenas, and Nicolaus, a proselyte of Antioch. These they set before the apostles, and they prayed and laid hands on them. (Acts 6:1–6)

The need for the Seven to be chosen arose from growth in the church. As the church grew, there arose more spiritual and physical needs among the new converts. Widows, for example, were usually dependent on others for their daily needs. One problem that emerged in the early church was that the Greek-speaking Jewish widows were being neglected. When the twelve apostles received news of this problem, they knew that something must be done. They understood the importance of providing for the physical needs of the people. They understood that allowing this problem to continue could cause division in the church.

But there was another problem. Although the apostles realized the gravity of the situation before them, they also realized that for them to get distracted with serving tables would divert them from their primary calling of preaching the Word of God. The apostles were not indicating that it would be too humiliating for them to serve widows. Jesus had taught them that being a leader in His kingdom is very different from being a worldly leader (Matt. 20:25–27), and He had washed their feet to demonstrate servant leadership (John 13:1–18). Rather, the apostles wanted to remain faithful to the calling and the gifts they had received from God. For them to leave the preaching of the Word to serve tables would have been a mistake. Instead, they proposed a better solution to this problem.

The apostles decided to call all the disciples together and present a solution to the problem. The disciples were to choose seven men to be appointed to the task of overseeing the daily distribution of food. The members of the congregation, however, were not to simply choose anyone who was willing to serve, they had to select men who had a good reputation and were Spirit-filled. By appointing these men to help with the daily distribution of food, the apostles took this need seriously but did not get distracted from their primary calling. With the Seven appointed to take care of this problem, the apostles were able to devote themselves "to prayer and to the ministry of the word" (v. 4).

The primary spiritual leaders of the congregation were the apostles. They were appointed to a "ministry of the word." As the church grew, the number of problems grew with it. As a result, other factors began to distract them from their calling. The Seven were needed to allow the apostles the freedom to continue with their work. This is a similar paradigm to what we see with the offices of elder and deacon. Like the apostles, the elders' primary role is one of preaching the Word of God (Eph. 4:11; 1 Tim. 3:2; Titus 1:9). Like the Seven, deacons are needed to serve the congregation in meeting whatever needs may arise. Thus, although the term *deacon* does not occur in the Acts 6 passage, this passage provides a helpful model of how godly servants can assist those who are called to preach the Word of God. (Note: We must remember that the "preaching" we are referring to is much broader than standing behind a pulpit and delivering a sermon but would include discipleship and sharing God's Word in various settings.)

Surprisingly, the Greek term *diakonos* occurs only three or four times as a designation of an officeholder. The first occurrence is in Romans 16:1, where Phoebe is called a *diakonos* "of the church at Cenchreae." It is debated as to whether Paul is using the term *diakonos* here as a general term for "servant" or as a more technical term for a "deacon" (i.e., a church officer). Most English Bible versions choose the more neutral translation "servant," but the RSV renders it "deaconess," and the NRSV renders it "deacon."

The second occurrence of *diakonos* as a reference to a church office is found in Paul's opening greeting in his letter to the Philippians. He addresses "all the saints in Christ Jesus who are at Philippi, with the overseers and deacons" (Phil. 1:1). This is the only place where Paul greets church officers in the salutation of a letter and is perhaps the clearest indication of a distinction between church members and church leaders in Paul's early writings. The presence of such leaders, however, does not change Paul's writing style of addressing the entire congregation. Paul links the overseers and deacons with all the saints since they are not to be treated as believers on a higher level.

The final two occurrences of *diakonos* as a reference to a church office are found in 1 Timothy 3, where Paul lists the requirements for "deacons" (vv. 8, 12). It is striking that Paul does not explain the duties of this office, which suggests that the Ephesian church already had experience with deacons. Paul simply lists the qualifications and assumes the church will use these officers in the appropriate manner. The fact that deacons do not need to be "able to teach" is a feature that sets them apart from the elders (cf. 1 Tim. 3:2; 5:17). Because Paul does not list any of the duties deacons should perform, it is likely that the early church understood the Seven chosen in Acts 6 to be a model for their own ministry. That is, as deacons they were responsible for caring for the physical needs of the congregation and doing whatever was needed so that the elders could focus on their work of teaching and shepherding.

THE QUALIFICATIONS OF DEACONS

Unlike the qualifications for elders, which are found in two passages (1 Tim. 3:1–7; Titus 1:5–9), the only passage in Scripture that mentions the qualifications for deacons is 1 Timothy 3:8–13. The similarities of the qualifications for deacons and elders/overseers are striking in 1 Timothy 3.

Like an elder, a deacon must not be addicted to much wine (cf. 1 Tim. 3:3, "not a drunkard") or greedy for dishonest gain (cf. 1 Tim. 3:3, "not a lover of money"). He must be blameless (cf. 1 Tim. 3:2, which uses a different Greek term), the husband of one wife, and one who manages his children and household well. Furthermore, the focus of the qualifications is on the moral character of the person who is to fill the office—someone who is mature and whose behavior is above reproach. The main difference between an elder and a deacon is a difference of gifts and calling, not character.

In 1 Timothy 3, Paul gives an official, but not exhaustive, list of the requirements for deacons. Consequently, if a *moral* qualification is listed for elders but not for deacons, that qualification still applies to deacons. The same goes for those qualifications listed for deacons but not for elders. For example, simply because it is not listed in the requirements for elders, an elder is not permitted to be double-tongued (1 Tim. 3:8). Paul already stated that elders must be "above reproach," which would include this prohibition. The differences in the qualifications, then, signify traits that are either particularly fitting for the officeholder to possess in order to accomplish his duties or especially needed in light of particular problems in the location to which Paul writes (in this case Ephesus). Most likely, Paul is giving descriptions that counter the descriptions of the false teachers in Ephesus. Thus, these descriptions mostly involve personal characteristics, not duties. Because many of the requirements for deacons are the same as those for elders, we will focus here on the requirements that are unique to deacons.

Dignified (1 Tim. 3:8)

The first requirement Paul lists for deacons is that they must be dignified. The Greek word translated "dignified" (*semnos*) occurs only four times in the New Testament (Phil. 4:8; 1 Tim. 3:8, 11; Titus 2:2). The term normally refers to something that is honorable, respectable, esteemed, or worthy and is closely related to "respectable," which is given as a qualification for elders (1 Tim. 3:2). In Philippians 4:8, Paul exhorts the believers to meditate on things that are true, *honorable*, just, pure, lovely, commendable, excellent, and worthy of praise. In Titus 2:2, Paul commands the older men to be "dignified." The other two occurrences are found in 1 Timothy 3—one as a requirement for a deacon (v. 8) and the other for his wife (v. 11). Thus, a deacon and his wife must be characterized as people who are honored and respected by those who know them. The work of a deacon is service oriented. This does not mean, however, that the leadership a deacon provides is not important. Such work is often crucial to the life of the church and requires someone who is respected.

Not Double-Tongued (1 Tim. 3:8)

The second requirement is that a deacon must not be double-tongued. The Greek word (*dilogos*) literally means "something said twice," and it occurs only here in the New Testament. People who are "double-tongued" say one thing to certain people but something else to others, or they say one thing but mean another. They are two-faced and insincere. Their words cannot be trusted, and thus they lack credibility. Thus deacons must be those who speak the truth in love. They cannot be slippery with their words, seeking to manipulate situations for their own personal good.

Sound in Faith and Life (1 Tim. 3:9)

Paul also indicates that a deacon must "hold the mystery of the faith with a clear conscience" (1 Tim. 3:9). The reference to "the mystery of the faith" is another way for Paul to speak of the gospel (cf. 1 Tim. 3:16). Consequently, this statement refers to the doctrinal beliefs of a deacon. Unlike those who have suffered shipwreck regarding the faith (1 Tim. 1:19) and whose consciences are seared (1 Tim. 4:2), deacons are to hold firm to the true gospel without wavering. Yet this qualification does not merely involve one's beliefs, for he also must hold these beliefs "with a clear conscience." That is, the behavior of a deacon must be consistent with his beliefs. If it is not, his conscience will speak against him and condemn him. Thus, this requirement speaks not only to the doctrine of a deacon but also to his behavior. Similarly, Paul instructs older men to be "sound in faith" (Titus 2:2). False teachings were rampant in Ephesus and were reaping havoc in the church. Paul, therefore, stresses the need for deacons to be sound in their faith. One might think that this require-ment is not necessary because deacons are not respon-sible for teaching in the church. Yet, as church officers and leaders, they have influence on the lives and beliefs of others. Furthermore, simply because deacons are not required to teach does not mean they are not permitted to teach.

Tested (1 Tim. 3:10)

Another qualification not specifically mentioned in the list for elders is the need for deacons to be tested before they can serve the church in an official capacity. Paul writes, "And let them also be tested first; then let them serve as deacons if they prove themselves blameless" (1 Tim. 3:10). Paul states that those who prove themselves to be "blameless" are quali-fied to serve as deacons. This is a general term referring to the overall character of a person's life (cf. Titus 1:6, where the same word is used) and is similar to the word used for the qualification of elders in 1 Timothy 3:2 ("above reproach").

Although Paul does not specify what type of testing is to take place, at a minimum, the candidate's personal background, reputation, and theological positions should be examined. But not only should the moral, spiritual, and doctrinal aspects be tested, the congregation also must consider the person's actual service in the church. A person with a deacon's heart is one who looks for opportunities to serve. As a person is given more responsibilities in the church, his ability to serve in a responsible manner and his ability to relate to others should be examined. Allowing someone who has not been tested to become a deacon can lead to many problems later. As with the elders, time is needed to assess the candidate because the sins of some are not immediately apparent (1 Tim. 3:6; 5:24). Thus, a hasty appointment to office is unwise and contrary to the intent of the qualifications. A specific length of time, however, is not given and should be left up to the local church to decide.

Godly Wife (1 Tim. 3:11)

It is debated whether this verse refers to the wife of a deacon or to a deaconess. For the sake of the discussion, we will assume the verse is speaking about the qualifications of a deacon's wife. According to Paul, the wives of deacons must "be dignified, not slanderers, but sober-minded, faithful in all things." First, like her husband, the wife must be dignified, or respectable. Second, she must not be a slanderer or a person who goes around spreading gossip. Later, Paul warns younger widows to remarry so that they do not learn to become idle, "going about from house to house, and not only idlers, but also gossips and busybodies, saying what they should not" (1 Tim. 5:13; cf. 2 Tim. 3:3; Titus 2:3). A deacon's wife also must be sober-minded, or temperate. The same word is used for elders in 1 Timothy 3:2. That is, she must be able to make good judgments and must not be involved in things that might hinder such judgment. Finally, she must be "faithful in all things" (cf. 1 Tim. 5:10). This requirement is general in nature and functions similarly to the requirement for elders to be "above reproach" (1 Tim. 3:2; Titus 1:6) or for deacons to be "blameless" (1 Tim. 3:10). The wife of a deacon must be a trustworthy person. The character of a deacon's wife is important to the success of his ministry. She must be committed, self-controlled, and faithful like her husband. Paul does not mention that the wives first must be tested, however, since it is not they, but their husbands, who are appointed to the office.

The character of a potential deacon and his wife should be examined before he is put into office. The high standard for deacons should not be minimized simply because they do not normally teach or lead the church. As officers of the church, they represent the church in some capacity, handling important and sometimes sensitive tasks.

THE ROLE OF DEACONS

Whereas the office of elder is often ignored in the modern church, the office of deacon is often misunderstood. In many churches, the board of deacons provides the spiritual leadership in the church in partnership with the pastor. They are involved in making the important decisions of the church and often are involved in teaching and shepherding. But based on the New Testament data, the role of the deacon is mainly a servant role. Deacons are needed in the church to provide logistical and material support so that the elders can concentrate their effort on the Word of God and prayer.

Different from Elders

The New Testament does not provide much information concerning the role of deacons. The requirements given in

1 Timothy 3:8–12 focus on the deacon's character and family life. There are, however, some clues as to the function of deacons when their requirements are compared with those of the elders. Although many of the qualifications are the same or very similar, there are some notable differences.

Perhaps the most noticeable distinction between elders and deacons is that deacons do not need to be "able to teach" (1 Tim. 3:2). Deacons are called to "hold" to the faith with a clear conscience, but they are not called to "teach" that faith (1 Tim. 3:9). This suggests that the deacons do not have an official teaching role in the church. Again, this does not mean that deacons cannot teach in any capacity but simply that they are not called to teach or preach as a matter of responsibility related to their office as deacon.

Like elders, deacons must manage their house and children well (1 Tim. 3:4, 12). But when referring to deacons, Paul does not compare managing one's household to taking care of God's church (1 Tim. 3:5). The reason for this omission is most likely due to the fact that deacons are not given a ruling or leading position in the church—a function that belongs to the elders.

Although Paul indicates that a person must be tested before he can hold the office of deacon (1 Tim. 3:10), the requirement that he cannot be a new convert is not included. Paul notes that if an elder is a recent convert "he may become puffed up with conceit" (1 Tim. 3:6). One implication of this distinction could be that those who hold the office of elder—because they possess leadership over the church—are more susceptible to pride. On the contrary, it is not as likely for a deacon—someone who is in more of a servant role—to fall into this same sin.

The fact that Paul includes the character of a deacon's wife also might reveal an important distinction (1 Tim. 3:11).

Because the role of a deacon is focused toward serving and not leading, a wife could more easily be involved in his ministry. The wife of an elder would be more limited since Paul forbids women "to teach or to exercise authority over a man" (1 Tim. 2:12). Finally, the title "overseer" (1 Tim. 3:2) implies general oversight over the spiritual well-being of the congregation, whereas the title "deacon" implies one who has a service-oriented ministry.

Duties of Deacons

We have discussed some distinctions between elders and deacons, but we have yet to specify the precise duties of deacons. We already have indicated that deacons are not responsible for teaching or leading the congregation. They are not the spiritual leaders of the church. Instead, the deacons provide leadership over the service-oriented functions of the church. The Bible, however, does not clearly indicate the function of deacons. But based on the pattern established in Acts 6 with the apostles and the Seven, it seems best to view the deacons as servants who do whatever is necessary to allow the elders to accomplish their God-given calling of shepherding and teaching the church. Just as the apostles delegated administrative responsibilities to the Seven, so the elders are to delegate responsibilities to the deacons so that the elders can focus their efforts elsewhere. As a result, each local church is free to define the tasks of deacons based on their particular needs.

What are some duties that deacons might be responsible for today? Basically they could be responsible for any item not related to teaching and ruling the church. Below is a list of possible duties.

- *Facilities*. The deacons could be responsible for the basic management of the church property. This would include making sure the place of worship is prepared for the worship service. Other items may include cleanup, sound system, etc.

- *Benevolence.* Similar to what took place in Acts 6:1–6 with the daily distribution to the widows, the deacons should be involved in administrating funds to the needy.

- *Finances.* Some believe that matters of finance should be handled by the elders since the famine-relief money brought by Paul and Barnabas was delivered to the elders (Acts 11:30). But while the elders can oversee the financial business of the church, it is probably best left to the deacons to handle the day-to-day matters. This would include collecting and counting the offering, record keeping, helping to set the church budget, etc.

- *Ushers.* The deacons could be responsible for distributing bulletins, seating the congregation, preparing the elements for communion, etc.

- *Logistics.* Deacons should be available to help in a variety of ways so that the elders are able to concentrate on teaching and shepherding the church.

THE DISTINCTION BETWEEN ELDERS AND DEACONS

The relationship between the office of elder and the office of deacon is often assumed but rarely articulated. In this section we will analyze the New Testament data and seek to answer the question of whether the deacons hold a lower office than the elders, and, if so, how the two offices should relate to each other.

Deacon Is a Lower Office

There are a number of factors in Scripture that indicate that the office of deacon is, in one sense, a lesser office than that of elder. First, the function of the deacons is to provide support for the elders so that they can continue their work without being distracted by other matters. Just as the apostles appointed seven men to care for the physical needs of the congregation in the daily distribution of food (Acts 6:1–6), so the deacons are needed so that the elders can attend to the spiritual needs of the congregation. The title "deacon" also suggests one who has a secondary role as one who comes beside and assists others. Deacons are not involved in the important tasks of teaching (cf. 1 Tim. 3:2; 5:17; Titus 1:9) and shepherding (cf. Acts 20:28; Eph. 4:11; 1 Peter 5:1–2). These tasks are reserved mainly for the elders. Rather, the deacons are needed to provide assistance and support so that the work of the church can continue effectively and smoothly.

Second, the office of deacon is mentioned after the office of elder/overseer. There are two examples in the New Testament. In Philippians 1:1, Paul not only greets the entire congregation (as was his normal practice), but he also greets the "overseers and deacons." Later, when Paul lists the needed qualifications for overseers and deacons in 1 Timothy 3, the qualifications for overseers are listed first. Although such ordering does not necessarily indicate order of priority, it at least may emphasize the importance of those who teach and lead the church.

Third, references to the office of deacon are far less frequent than references to the office of elder. Although the general use of the Greek term *diakonos* occurs quite frequently, the more specific use of the term as a reference to an officeholder is found only three or four times in the New Testament (Rom. 16:1[?]; Phil. 1:1; 1 Tim. 3:8, 12). On the other hand, the terms for elder and overseer as references to officeholders occur more than twenty times. Again, these numbers are not conclusive by themselves, but they add to the point that deacons held a lesser office.

Fourth, elders were appointed to new churches before deacons were. The early church in Jerusalem had elders before they had deacons—assuming the Seven appointed in Acts 6 could not technically be considered "deacons." During Paul's first missionary journey, he and Barnabas appointed elders in the church of Asia Minor (Acts 14:23). Yet, nowhere does Luke indicate that deacons were appointed. While this omission does not prove that deacons did not exist in the churches at that time, the fact that they are not mentioned indicates that they were not as important to the progress of the gospel in the mind of Luke. Later, Paul commands Titus to appoint elders in every city on the island of Crete (Titus 1:5), but he says nothing about deacons. If deacons were as important to the life of the church, it would seem that he also would have included instructions to appoint deacons and included the needed qualifications as he did in 1 Timothy.

Deacon Is a Distinct Office

There is some danger in describing the office of deacon as a lower office than the office of elder. Misconceptions concerning the two offices are common, so it is important to clarify what was not intended in our previous discussion. For example, there is no indication in Scripture that the office of deacon is a lower office in the sense that one must become a deacon before he can serve as an elder. These offices are distinguished by their function in the church and the gifts of the individual. Similar, yet distinct, qualifications are given for elders and for deacons. Paul does not indicate in his qualifications for elders that one first must have been a deacon. As a matter of fact, his comment that an elder must not be a recent convert (1 Tim. 3:6) would make little sense if he expected a person to be a deacon before he could move up to the position of an elder. Furthermore, it is likely that many churches did not have deacons at the beginning of their existence. The distinction between elders and deacons is not a distinction of rank but a distinction of function. Unlike elders, deacons do not teach and shepherd the congregation (1 Tim. 3:2, 5). If a person is a gifted teacher and meets the qualifications listed in 1 Timothy 3:1–7, he should seek to become an elder. On the other hand, if someone does not have the gift of teaching but enjoys serving in other areas, he might consider becoming a deacon. Becoming a deacon is not a stepping-stone to becoming an elder. The two offices are distinct in that they require different kinds of people.

Deacons are also distinct from elders in the sense that they are not merely the personal assistants of the elders. Deacons are not called to serve the elders. Rather, they are called to serve the church. The Seven in Acts 6 were not enlisted to serve the apostles. They were selected and appointed to help solve a critical issue in the life of the congregation. Although it is necessary for the elders to work closely with the deacons, the deacons are not there simply to answer to the call of the elders but should be given freedom to serve the church. Moreover, it is inappropriate for the deacons to be chosen only by the elders. The congregation as a whole should be involved in the process. Again, the reason is that the deacons do not exist to serve the elders but are called to serve the entire congregation.

Deacon Is an Important Office

To say that the office of deacon is, in some senses, a lower office than the office of elder is not to minimize its importance in the life and health of the church. The appointing of the seven men in Acts 6 could have saved the church from potential disaster. Because the Hellenistic widows were being overlooked by the church, some Hellenistic Jews may have been tempted to form their own congregations. The result would have been devastating to the unity of the church. Thus, what began as a minor issue could have turned into a massive problem if left unchecked. The church could have experienced its first split and been stifled in its progress to proclaim the gospel message to all the nations. Wisely, however, the apostles appointed the Seven to solve this problem. In a similar manner, deacons are needed in the church to care for the "physical" life of the church.

Neither are deacons less than elders in the sense that they are lesser Christians or are lesser in God's eyes. All gifts are from God and are given according to His will (1 Cor. 12:11). Paul uses the analogy of a body to illustrate the point that all members that make up a body are needed. The foot, hand, eye, and ear—although they have different functions—are all integral parts of the body and cannot be ignored. As a matter of fact, Paul states that those who receive less honor because of their gifts and use in the church, should not be neglected. He states,

> The parts of the body that seem to be weaker are indispensable, and on those parts of the body that we think less honorable we bestow the greater honor, and our unpresentable parts are treated with greater modesty, which our more presentable parts do not require. But God has so composed the body, giving greater honor to the part that

lacked it, that there may be no division in the body, but that the members may have the same care for one another. (1 Cor. 12:22–25)

CONCLUSION

Elders are needed in every church because deacons are not given the task of leading and teaching the congregation. The seven men chosen in Acts 6, while not specifically called "deacons," provide the closest parallel to the Christian office. Just as the Seven were needed to attend to the physical needs of the Greek-speaking Jewish widows, so deacons are needed to look after the physical needs of the church. Whereas elders are charged with the tasks of teaching and leading the church, deacons are given a more service-oriented function. That is, they are given the task of taking care of matters related more to the physical or temporal concerns of the church. By being responsible for the oversight of such concerns, the diaconal work allows the elders to focus their efforts on shepherding the spiritual needs of the congregation. But while deacons are not called to lead the church, this does not mean that they do not have to meet the biblical qualifications. The character of a potential deacon and his wife should be examined before he is put into office. Although Scripture seems to indicate that the office of deacon is a secondary office to that of the elder, the role of the deacons is vital to the life and health of the church.

Select Bibliography

Brand, Chad Owen, and R. Stanton Norman. *Perspectives on Church Government: Five Views of Church Polity.* Nashville: Broadman and Holman, 2004.

Dever, Mark. *Nine Marks of a Healthy Church.* Wheaton, IL: Crossway, 2000.

Dever, Mark, and Paul Alexander. *The Deliberate Church: Building Your Ministry on the Gospel.* Wheaton, IL: Crossway, 2005.

Engle, Paul E., and Steven B. Cowan, eds. *Who Runs the Church? 4 Views on Church Government.* Grand Rapids: Zondervan, 2004.

Hammett, John S. *Biblical Foundations for Baptist Churches: A Contemporary Ecclesiology.* Grand Rapids: Kregel, 2005.

Merkle, Benjamin L. *40 Questions About Elders and Deacons.* Grand Rapids: Kregel, 2008.

Newton, Phil A. *Elders in Congregational Life: Rediscovering the Biblical Model for Church Leadership.* Grand Rapids: Kregel, 2005.

Piper, John. *Biblical Eldership.* Minneapolis: Desiring God Ministries, 1999.

Strauch, Alexander. *Biblical Eldership: An Urgent Call to Restore Biblical Church Leadership.* Revised and expanded. Littleton, CO: Lewis and Roth, 1995.

Scripture Index